Unpacking The Kingdom Of Heaven

Cycle A Sermons for Proper 17
Through Thanksgiving
Based On The Gospel Texts

Peter Andrew Smith

CSS Publishing Company, Inc.
Lima, Ohio

FIRST EDITION
Copyright © 2022
by CSS Publishing Co., Inc.

Library of Congress Cataloging-in-Publication Data:

Names: Smith, Peter Andrew, author.
Title: Unpacking the kingdom of heaven : cycle A sermons for proper 17-29 based on the gospel texts / Peter Andrew Smith.
Description: Lima, Ohio : CSS Publishing Company, Inc., 2022.
Identifiers: LCCN 2022027087 (print) | LCCN 2022027088 (ebook) | ISBN 9780788030529 (paperback) | ISBN 9780788030536 (adobe pdf)
Subjects: LCSH: Bible. Matthew--Sermons. | Pentecost season--Sermons. | Common lectionary (1992)
Classification: LCC BS2575.54 .S65 2022 (print) | LCC BS2575.54 (ebook) | DDC 226.2/06--dc23/eng/20220810
LC record available at https://lccn.loc.gov/2022027087
LC ebook record available at https://lccn.loc.gov/2022027088

Unless otherwise noted, all scriptures are from the WORLD ENGLISH BIBLE, public domain.

For more information about CSS Publishing Company resources, visit our website at www.csspub.com, email us at csr@csspub.com, or call (800) 241-4056.

e-book:
ISBN-13: 978-0-7880-3053-6
ISBN-10: 0-7880-3053-1

ISBN-13: 978-0-7880-3052-9
ISBN-10: 0-7880-3052-3

PRINTED IN USA

Contents

Being In The Right Place

"Get behind me, Satan!" is easy to understand. Even if we aren't sure where or why the phrase appears in the Bible, the meaning is straightforward. Someone evil is blocking the way and they need to move, to go somewhere else, so we can go forward. Understanding the phrase is helpful because it allows us to hear the lesson this morning at a deeper level as we seek to understand not merely the words but what they mean for our lives and our faith.

The gospel lesson from Matthew 16:21-28 comes immediately after the passage where Jesus asked the disciples who others said he was and let them answer about what the crowds and people were speculating about him. Jesus followed that question by asking the disciples who they said he was and Peter, of course, professed Jesus to be the Messiah, the Christ, sent from God to bring about the salvation so desperately needed by the world. Jesus praised Peter, telling him those words meant that God was working in his life to show him the truth that he needed to know and experience.

The conversation continues with Jesus teaching and explaining to the disciples what it meant for him to be the Christ. He talked about his upcoming suffering, his rejection, and his death to fulfill what God wanted and needed. He talked of the leadership and respected people in Jerusalem hating him. As Jesus talked we can almost imagine Peter fidgeting and squirming as the disciple listened. What Jesus taught wasn't the type of life and ministry and future that Peter wanted for Jesus or for himself so Peter took Jesus aside and rebuked him saying, "Far be it from you, Lord! This will never be done to you." (Matthew 16:22 WEB). We could hear the words Peter used a number of different ways except that the gospel writer told us that Peter *rebuked* Jesus and that clears up any question about what Peter was doing. The Greek word we translate as rebuke is the same word used when Jesus silenced evil spirits (Matthew 17:18) and when he stilled the storm (Matthew 8:26).

Peter wasn't saying something like, "O Jesus, that would be terrible if that would happen," as he tried to come to grips with what Jesus had taught. No, Peter was telling Jesus to be quiet and listen to him. The disciple was trying to correct the master by saying, "You can't do that. Those events must never happen." because Peter wasn't simply struggling with a difficult teaching — he was refusing to accept Jesus' words and told Jesus how he should act as the Messiah.

That is what provoked the harsh words from Jesus, "Get behind me, Satan! You are a stumbling block to me, for you are not setting your mind on the things of God, but on the things of men" (Matthew 16:23 WEB). Peter had realized Jesus was the Christ sent to bring about God's salvation but when Peter was told what the salvation looked like and how it was achieved, he rejected what Jesus said and intended to do.

There is no doubt that Jesus put Peter in his place by not merely reaffirming his teaching about what must happen to the Messiah but by declaring that Peter was becoming a stumbling block to him and denouncing Peter's focus on what the disciple wanted instead of being open to what God wants. While it would be simple to contrast the profession of Peter with this exchange and conclude that Peter got it right at the start and then got it wrong later on, I think the combination of the two lessons is a bit more profound than that.

Peter was inspired to know who Jesus was and what his role was in the plan of salvation. Peter had been open to God and had seen the salvation promised by the prophets in front of him. Peter had followed and he knew who Jesus was and had come to believe that God would remake the world through him. That is why Peter could profess Jesus as the Christ. The problem Peter had was that when he heard how that would happen, what had to take place in the life of Jesus, he could not accept it.

In other words, Peter realized that Jesus was the Christ come to save him and the world and Peter assumed that by knowing that, he understood everything he needed to understand about Jesus and the way God was opening through him. Peter thought he knew what the Messiah would do. The chosen one from God would triumph. The promised Christ would sweep aside opposition and show the world the power of God. The Savior would be victorious in ways that everyone would acknowledge and no one could deny. That meant that everything Jesus was saying flew in the face of what Peter knew and expected. Jesus talked about suffering and rejection, not triumph and acceptance. Jesus taught that he must die to be raised to glory instead of being raised to glory and living a long life. So it's really not surprising that Peter took Jesus aside and told him he was wrong about what it meant to be the Messiah.

For a moment let me skip past Jesus rebuking Peter and get to the sayings that follow where Jesus told the disciples that they had to pick up their crosses and follow and that anyone who tried to save their life would lose it and anyone who lost their life for Jesus' sake would save it. Because what was happening between Jesus and Peter points us to the reality of living as God's people when we pick up our cross and follow.

The cross is a strange symbol for our faith because before Jesus the cross was a symbol of terror and oppression. Crucifixion was the means by that the Romans cruelly flaunted their power and struck fear into the hearts of people. The cross was the ultimate symbol of death. A public means of spreading despair. Everyone nailed to a cross was a criminal in the eyes of Rome. Everyone killed on a cross died a humiliating and painful death. That was the cross that Jesus was nailed to at Calvary. Rome's answer to ensure things stayed the way they were. The power of fear and violence dominating the earth. That's why Jesus was killed on the cross — to publicly show that his ministry, his words, his life were being crushed by the power of violence and death. The cross is about the anguish of the disciples and the desolation of Good Friday and that is exactly what Jesus told us to take up and follow him with. A cross — a shape that once signified brutality and death. It is a symbol that reminds us of Jesus' suffering and death. In taking up the cross you cannot ignore Good Friday and how Jesus was betrayed and suffered and how the disciples despaired. You cannot ignore how Jesus died and was buried.

As Christians, the cross is the powerful reminder that the story of Jesus does not end with the tomb because when the women came on Easter the tomb was empty. Jesus who had died at Calvary was alive again. The power and promise of God stripped away the fear and despair of death for all time. That is why the cross is a symbol transformed by the power of God. The cross stands as a powerful reminder that the greatest evil the world can produce cannot overcome the mercy and love of God. Through the cross we see that God's love can bring life and joy from death and despair. Jesus dies upon the cross. Jesus rises from the dead. Jesus is alive. We carry with us the symbol of the cross as the ultimate reminder of the actions of Jesus, the power of God, the triumph of Easter.

Jesus said to his disciples to take up the cross (Matthew 16:24). There is still fear, despair, and violence in our world; that is why our carrying of the cross is so important. The cross is a sign to the world that God can heal the broken and that the power of grace can overcome the greatest failure. The cross is God's promise to the world that there is a better way, a better place, a greater purpose. God answers the pain and sorrow, the hurt, and the anguish of our world through the life death and resurrection of Jesus Christ.

That is why we are told to pick up our cross. We are to pick up the faith of our fathers and mothers. Pick up the hope and good news. Pick up the joy of God's place in your life. The cross is our symbol. It is a symbol of transformation and hope. It is a symbol of light spilling into the world and a symbol that God understands hardship, fear, and suffering. For as we pick up the cross, we come to see the world differently. Let me be clear that knowing, understanding, and coming to faith is not the end of the journey. Jesus never said, "I am the destination — come to me and your faith is finished." We don't realize that God is re-vealed to the world in Jesus and then never have to grow, devel-op and trust in God any longer. No, Jesus says, "Pick up your cross and follow."

We discover who we are and how we are supposed to live; we come to know God and God's call to us in Jesus by living as a disciple. The grace, the love, the mercy of God become real to us and show us things we never expected about ourselves and life as we walk as Jesus calls us to walk. We learn the path we are to take and the work God unfolds in our world through our service and our sacrifice. We realize the truth not in only in our heads but also in our hearts when we follow where Jesus leads.

That brings me back to Jesus telling Peter to get behind him. In part that was to get Peter out of the way so that Jesus could move forward and do what he needed to do. But more impor-tantly, I think it was to get Peter where he needed to be. The truth is that you can't learn from Jesus if you are trying to get Jesus to do what *you* want. You can't grow in faith if you are not looking to walk in the footsteps of the Savior of the world. You can only experience the life Jesus brings by following. You can only dis-cover the truth Jesus shares by being humble. You can only find the way Jesus opens by setting your mind and heart by being a disciple.

It is important to not be a hindrance to what God is doing in the world. We need to recognize how in our lives sometimes we get in the way of what God is doing, we block the Holy Spir-it from working through us, we are a hindrance to the gospel. When we realize those things and times in our lives we need to repent and change where we are, in order to be the people God calls us to be and that happens when we put aside what we want, what we expect, what we think should happen, and listen, learn, and experience what God is bringing about. Ultimately that is what Jesus meant when he told us to pick up our crosses and to be ready to let go of our lives for his sake.

Pick up your cross and follow. Listen and watch for God in your life and let your faith grow. Love and serve others because that is the life Jesus calls you to live. Know that when you are laying down your life and not struggling to hold onto things and desires and expectations, you will discover the richness and promise of the salvation that Jesus gives to us through his death and resurrection.

Amen.

Proper 18 (23)
Matthew 18:15-20

The Test Of Christian Love

"For where two or three are gathered together in my name, there I am in the middle of them" (Matthew 18:20 WEB). The last verse of the gospel lesson is a familiar and comforting passage of scripture. Jesus' words serve as a reminder that whenever a group of believers worship, pray, and serve that the spirit of Christ is present and I certainly believe that to be true. When we come together in Jesus' name something special happens and our gathering is more than simply you and me for within our midst is the spirit and presence of the living God. That is affirming and heartening for us within the church. We can expect to feel the movement of the Spirit in worship and celebration and even in our outreach work.

Yet the focus of our gospel lesson isn't on the Spirit being with us when we come to worship but during a more surprising time. The verse where Jesus promises to be with us comes at the conclusion of a passage that begins, "If your brother sins against you..." (Matthew 18:15 WEB) and discusses how to deal with conflict and that isn't a coincidence but rather something important for us to understand. Jesus commands us to love one another as he loves us and through his life, Jesus demonstrates those words as he welcomes the outcasts, blesses those in need, and proclaims the grace and mercy of God through the cross. As Christians we follow the example and the way of Jesus, so we seek to love as Jesus loves and care for those around us as Jesus cares and at times that becomes a struggle for us, especially when we face difficult people and hurtful situations. For the test of Christian love is how we act when it is hard for us to love and there is perhaps no time more difficult for us to show Christian love than when someone has hurt us.

It would be nice if I could tell you that those things never happen between people in the church but the truth is that Jesus calls us, flawed as we are, with our pride, our opinions, our pain, our anger, our fears, and everything else that we have within us. When we draw close to one another in faith there are times when we hurt each another. When I say that, I'm not speaking directly about any issue in particular or any situation within a specific congregation or denomination. I'm speaking from the gospel about what happens within the church and within our lives. It can take place in any church or gathering of believers in the world. It can happen in our personal lives with friends and family. Someone we trust hurts us. Someone we are connected to causes us pain. Please notice that I said, "what happens within the church and within our lives" and not "what might happen" because we will have some sort of quarrel, dispute, argument, difficulty, or whatever else we call it with those around us at some point. It is a situation that everyone and anyone can find themselves in. Tempers will flare, words will be spoken, actions will be taken, and we will feel hurt, angry, and upset. We will find it difficult to love those who have done such a thing. As the writer GK Chesterton once pointed out, "Jesus commands us to love our neighbor and to love our enemy because often they are the same person."

When that person close to us hurts us, we have a problem because when we feel bitter, angry, resentful, and wish them harm we've stopped loving them. When what happened between us and another person makes us lose friends, reject family, foster hard feelings, and start to wonder how we can possibly be in the same room with the person, then we need to do something. Because with those emotions building within our hearts we have stopped being witnesses to grace and mercy. We cannot follow Jesus when our hearts are filled with hate and hurt. The gospel describes what we should do to try to reconcile, to rebuild the relationship, and to move past the emotions and situation. When we have been hurt, we may feel there is nothing we should do. After all, we're the ones who have been wronged. We may believe it is the other person's responsibility to come to us, but as people commanded to love we are to reach out and seek reconciliation and bring peace within our relationships.

The first step we take in love is to talk to the other person. Many problems with other people come about because we think they said something or felt something or did something when in fact they did not. So often all it takes for us to reconcile is to speak to the person and allow them to speak to us. I want to repeat that once more because I think we often don't want to take this step because none of us like confrontation. Yet Jesus tells us that the first step we need to take with someone we disagree with or have a problem with, is to talk to them. We need to talk and listen in order to correct misunderstandings and ensure that questions are asked, perspectives are shared, and people are heard. Quite honestly many times when the other person hears that what they have done has hurt us they will ask for forgiveness and sincerely apologize. It happens quite often.

The truth is though, that sometimes talking to the person goes nowhere. That is when we are told to get one or two others and go back to try and solve the problem. That may sound strange but remember a couple of things. The Bible talks about the need for two or three people to give testimony (Deuteronomy 19:15) because we often require different perspectives to help us see the truth. How many times have we had a disagreement with someone and believed we were in the right but when a third party tells us we are wrong then we reconsider? That is why, at this point, we are told to bring one or two others into the conversation. We don't simply bring people who will agree with us and whatever we say but rather bring someone to listen and share themselves.

We need someone who perhaps can help us see the situation with a fresh set of eyes and hear with a new pair of ears. Sometimes that is all is required to help both people see what is going on. Two or three witnesses don't make it a vote on what is right or wrong but help us gain a wider perspective and better understand what is happening. They also help us keep the holy inside this conflict that has become more difficult to resolve because remember that verse where Jesus talks about being with two or three gathered in faith? The point of bringing in a couple of people is to keep God in the situation. If you can't work out the dispute one on one chances are it gets deeper and more personal quickly and having someone calm things down, allowing peace and grace to rule in what is unfolding is, literally, a godsend. Much of the time that is all that is needed.

Sometimes we agree to disagree, we mend fences, we figure out a way to move past the argument or slight. Occasionally a more formal process of dispute resolution is needed and that is okay as well. We have those mechanisms in place in churches as most large organizations do for sometimes the wisdom and patience, the experience and the skills of the whole church need to be brought to bear on what is happening. Again that does not magically wipe away what took place but it can set us on the path to reconciliation. The words of someone from outside the dispute can help us to see everything in a new light. Perhaps showing us what we haven't seen or perhaps speaking the words to help the other person know how they have been wrong.

Yet sometimes even that is not enough. Despite talking and involving others no reconciliation has taken place and here the gospel lesson tells us to take it to the church. Again, I think we need to be aware the intention is not to have lots of people tell the other person they are wrong and we are right. The intention is and remains through this whole process to reconcile. We need to come back together. We need to make a new relationship where the old one has broken down and there are times when we need the moral authority of the church to encourage and support that happening. Sometimes that is required.

Yet the reality is that sometimes that is not enough and despite all of those things the person refuses to admit a wrong they have done and refuses to change their ways. At that point we are told "...let him be to you as a gentile or a tax collector" (Matthew 18:17b WEB). In other words let that person be as an outsider or someone who behaves in unacceptable ways. Gentiles were outside the faith, and tax collectors in the ancient world acted in a way that everyone recognized was dishonest and evil.

Yet I believe those words also point us back to Jesus because before we leap to the conclusion that we should shun and despise those we cannot reconcile with let's keep in mind the one speaking these words. Jesus welcomed the tax collectors and Gentiles in his ministry and offered them the grace and love of God in his actions and his words. He taught that they were children of God and worthy of the salvation he brought to the earth. Yet he never did the things they were known for — rejecting God and cheating people and that is the distinction we are to make as well. So with these words we are not given license to hate those we cannot reconcile with but rather we are encouraged to approach them as people who need to hear and see the good news of Jesus Christ. We treat those people with respect and we love them but we do not use their behavior or words as a model for our speech or action. We take the high road and we look to the time when we can reconcile.

For all through the gospel passage is the understanding that how we are to treat one another is with the grace and mercy of Christ leading us and shaping our words and behavior. We want God to be with us when we come to worship and pray and we look to know God's wisdom and strength to lead us when we are hurting and needing healing for ourselves and our relationships. Paul in one of his letters gives this advice to keep our conscience clear and "...let your way of life be worthy of the Good News of Christ" (Philippians 1:27 WEB). When we gather in Christ's name, we are assured of the presence of the divine among us and we ask God to guide us so that we can become people who do not merely speak about grace and love but show the meaning of those words with our lives.

We are never given permission to hurt and revile anyone for what they have done. Not when we first disagree, not when others try to help us sort things out, and not even when we are unable to reconcile. We are to love them. We can refuse to be a part of what they are doing, we can protect ourselves from their behavior and words, we can separate ourselves from them but we are not to hate them. We are to love them as Jesus loved those who had not heard and those who had not responded to God. For we are commanded to love others …period. Whether we get along with them or whether we do not, the call and the command are the same. We are to live with love as the basis of our actions and words. How we treat those we cannot reconcile with or even get along with is a powerful statement of our faithfulness in following the one who loved even those who crucified him. Our love for one another, especially those who have wronged us, is our strongest witness to God in the world.

Amen.

The Power Of Forgiveness

I was once discussing the story of Joseph and his brothers to an uninterested group of boys (Genesis 37-44). I asked what they thought Joseph did when his brothers came before him when he was in charge of Egypt.

One boy announced, "He remembered every single thing they ever did to him and man did he give it to them."

"You've got some of it right," I said. "He did remember every single thing they ever did to him and then the Bible says that he forgave them."

You could hear a pin drop as they thought about that and then the discussion really heated up.

Forgiveness has a power that cannot be denied. Being forgiven lifts the weight of shame and guilt from our shoulders. Forgiving another person permits us to move past old hurts and leave behind pain and anguish. Forgiveness allows relationships to start again and new beginnings to happen. Forgiveness renews and remakes our world.

I want to be clear about what I am talking about because sometimes we say forgiveness when we really mean forgetting or excusing and they are not the same things. Forgetting means not remembering that something happened. If you ask someone to forget you are asking them to live as if no harm was ever done and no pain was ever felt. In effect you want to pretend that the wrong never took place. That is forgetting.

Forgiveness on the other hand involves both people understanding and recognizing the pain and suffering that was caused. To forgive someone they have to admit they have hurt you. To be forgiven means accepting the burden of your wrong and having that taken away by another person. That also makes forgiveness very different from excusing. Excusing is providing a reason or a rationale for why something happened. An excuse means that there was a good reason or that the person who did the wrong had no real choice. An excuse seeks to take away responsibility and blame.

Forgiveness in contrast involves accepting blame. You ask forgiveness because you were wrong. You offer forgiveness knowing full well the other person is responsible for what you have experienced. Forgiveness then requires us to be aware of the hurt and pain that has happened and demands that we acknowledge the wrong that has taken place and understand who is responsible. We understand all of that is important because if we try to deny that someone was hurt, if we pretend no one is to blame, then we are not talking about forgiveness and we are not permitting the power of that new beginning to happen within us and our relationships.

As well, I think there is something else about forgiveness that is important for us to recognize. Forgiveness is simple. All you have to do is take responsibility and ask to be forgiven. All you have to do is listen to someone ask and agree to forgive. Forgiveness is simple but forgiveness is not easy. If we have wronged another, we have to accept responsibility. We have to admit that we are to blame, that we caused the suffering, that we are the guilty party, and that is why it is so important to understand the difference between forgiveness, excusing and forgetting. For all too often we try to make excuses, we try to escape the blame. Just listen to most public apologies made by politicians or celebrities caught cheating. They usually begin by saying they were wrong but then try to explain away their behavior or say it is not important. That is not asking for forgiveness, that is providing excuses or wishing people would forget a misdeed.

I say that it is hard to ask for forgiveness because it makes us vulnerable. We have to admit that we did something that we should not have done and we hurt another person. We have to place ourselves at their mercy. That is simple to do but it is certainly not easy. It is also hard to offer forgiveness to someone else because we have to let go of our anger, our moral superiority and choose not to punish the other person. The words "I forgive you" are simple to say but actually forgiving takes time and sometimes even effort on our part. It is never easy because inside of us we want the other person to feel the pain we are feeling and often we have trouble letting go of what happened. We feel we deserve or need to make the other person suffer for what they have done and as a result we hold onto the pain and grief. Forgiveness is not easy yet the Bible commands us to do just that for a very important reason because forgiveness is at the heart of what God has done through Jesus and the cross.

In Matthew 18:21-35, Jesus taught about forgiveness and told a parable that challenges us to see the power of forgiveness. We are reminded within those verses that forgiveness is not an option but a requirement of faith. We are told that we are to forgive just as we have been forgiven. We are warned that unless we forgive others we ourselves cannot experience forgiveness. I'm going to talk about those three things in this sermon but as I do I want us all to be aware that Jesus never says that we are to forgive and forget because quite honestly forgetting destroys the power of what forgiveness makes possible.

Peter came to Jesus with what seemed like a simple question. "Lord, how often shall my brother sin against me, and I forgive him? Until seven times?" (Matthew 18:21 WEB) and notice that Peter said, "my brother." That's important because honestly as we go through life we forgive people all the time. People who cut us off in the grocery store, who interrupt us when we are speaking, who telephone when we are busy, and we don't give those times a second thought. When a stranger walks in front of us it may be rude but we're not hurt. When someone speaks when we are speaking that rarely cuts us to the heart, and when we're drawn away from what we are doing we may grumble but we roll with it. Yet when a family member lies to us, betrays us, turns on us, when someone we love ignores us that is a different matter because when a family member, someone we are vulnerable with and look to for love, hurts us that cuts to the heart. When Peter said "my brother" he was asking Jesus about real meaningful things — not petty annoyances and he wanted to know how often. He gave what I expect he thought was a generous answer — an answer that was beyond expectations. He asked if you should forgive someone not once, not twice, but seven times and Jesus told him no.

Jesus said that the number is more like 77 or 7 times 7 depending on how you read the Greek. That isn't actually a number you should keep track of but another way for Jesus to say not to count the number of times you forgive but simply forgive. Let go of your anger, your rage, your pain. Refuse to allow what the other person has done to you to change who you are. Don't hold onto the hurt and relive it time and time again. Nowhere did Jesus say forget about what they have done.That is important because forgiveness is the way we release the pain, the hurt of the past, and refuse to allow what someone has done to keep hurting us. The only way that can happen, the only way it takes place is when we know what the other person did, when they understand what they have done, and we choose to not let that event, that action hurt us any longer in our lives. We remember what they have done, we do not forget, but we choose to make that action unimportant by forgiving.

That is not easy at times. That's why Jesus elsewhere told us to pray for those who hurt us (Matthew 5:44) because we usually need God's help to forgive others. That's why Jesus taught about the importance of forgiveness because it is a decision as well as being a process. It is where we let God show us how to heal our lives, release our burdens, and rebuild a relationship.

That brings us to the parable. It is a story about a servant who owed a tremendous debt. Jesus told us that the man owed 10,000 years of wages to the king and the debt was called due. The king wanted what was owed to him and the man begged for forgiveness. The king chose to forgive the man and wiped away the debt the man owed him.

The fact is that when someone hurts you there is only one way to make it right. You can't hurt them and balance the scales because if you do then you have two hurting people focused on revenge. You can't ignore the hurt, or pretend it never happened, because it did. The only thing that allows you to move forward, to change your life is to forgive them. That is what the king did in the parable. He forgave and the man began a new life that he never expected to have. He was free. The king had given him a gift that wais truly beyond measure.

Yet when the servant who had been forgiven ran into someone who owed him a small debt, the forgiven servant demanded repayment and the one who owed begged for mercy and time. Honestly the debt the man owed was quite small, almost insignificant compared to the debt the forgiven servant owed the king. But the servant the king forgave refused to offer the one indebted to him mercy and had the debtor taken away for punishment.

That is when the king heard and demanded the forgiven servant appear before him and explain himself. That does not end well for the forgiven yet unforgiving servant as the king then did something disturbing. He reinstated the original unpayable debt and sent the servant to be punished.

The end of the parable is shocking to hear because we expect that when the servant was forgiven by the king that was the end of the debt and honestly that would be the case if the king forgot about the debt or excused it. Then the debt would be simply gone as if it never existed or the servant would have no responsibility for it but remember the debt was forgiven not forgotten. That meant that the king released the servant to begin a new life. Free from his burden, the servant was expected, and dare I say was required, to be a different person but he wasn't. He hadn't learned anything from his second chance. He didn't understand that being forgiven meant extending that same mercy to others because you can not be forgiven if you do not forgive.

Let me stay with that point for a moment because I want to be clear about what Jesus was saying in the parable. He was not saying you can't be forgiven if you find it hard to forgive someone else because the truth is that forgiveness is hard. Jesus wasn't saying you can't be forgiven if you try to forgive but find yourself still angry and hurt because more than likely that will happen as you work your way to forgiveness. No, what Jesus taught in the parable was that you can't be forgiven if you simply refuse to forgive, refuse to try, refuse to let the forgiveness you have received make a difference in your life and extend that same grace to others.

That brings me back to why you can't forgive and forget because when you have been forgiven you need to let that change you. You need to let that grace, that gift you can't earn or get any other way, you need to let that into your life and be changed and then you need to give that same gift to others because that is the only way to let power of forgiveness work in your life and in your relationships. For the power of forgiveness isn't in erasing the past but rather in showing us the way to get through the pain and hurt. Forgiveness isn't about saying that something never happened but in living so the wrong, the pain no longer changes who we are.

We don't forget because we understand that there is something stronger and more powerful in our lives than the wounds and wrongs that others do. It is so that we know that God's gift to us in the cross is just that, a gift. It is given because of God's mercy, that allows us a new life because Jesus was crucified and risen to show us that nothing is stronger than God's love.

Let the forgiveness of God into your life. There is nothing that God cannot and will not forgive because no matter how bad our actions, our choices, our deeds, the fact is that God's love is greater and when we accept that forgiveness into our lives we discover that the way for us to live as God's people is to forgive. Forgiving others for what they have done, forgiving ourselves for not being perfect, and understanding the difference that forgiveness makes. This is especially so in a time like this when everyone is anxious and on edge. When we forgive others we live as Jesus calls us to live, we allow God to heal our lives, and we share God's grace with the world.

Amen.

Proper 20 (25)
Matthew 20:1-16

The Wonder Of God's Grace

"That's not fair!" was one of my favorite expressions when I was a teenager because like everyone else at that age I had a keenly tuned sense of outrage about injustice especially if something impacted my life. Usually when I said, "That's not fair!" to my mother she would take the time to explain to me how what she was expecting was fair because she expected the same from my brother or it was something everyone had to do. The day I said "You're not fair" to her though she came back with an answer that surprised me. "Of course I'm not fair," she replied. "I'm your mother and I love you." That, I admit, I didn't understand at the time because I assumed that if you loved someone fairness would be the most important thing.

Fairness or justice is important to all of us. We expect there to be a level playing field in life so that everyone has the same chances and opportunities, and that everyone is treated equally. Quite simply justice is when you get what you deserve. When you apply for a job you deserve to be considered and not to have things like skin color, sexual orientation, marital status, gender, or age influence the decision on whether you are hired or not. When you go into a store you deserve to be treated like everyone else and not be profiled. When the police need to be called you deserve to be protected not harassed or harmed.

Yet the truth is that justice is only the start because we also need mercy. We need to be forgiven when we make mistakes. We need to forgive others to heal relationships. If justice is getting what you deserve then mercy is when you don't get what you deserve. Like the debtor in the parable just before this in Matthew who was forgiven his debt (Matthew 18:21-35) sometimes we need mercy in our lives. As people of faith we believe and trust that mercy is what God offers us on the cross. We are not punished when we sin and repent but are rather forgiven and offered a new chance. We all want to live in a world where there is justice but we also need to experience mercy in that world. That brings me to talking about grace.

My mother wasn't fair to me because she was my mother and loved me. That meant that as well as justice and wanting me to have opportunities and not face injustice she also was forgiving when I did things wrong. Yes, there were consequences and sometimes punishments but at some point things were forgiven and life moved on but there was also something more. Since my mother loved me there were times that she made sure there were good things in my life that I didn't earn or deserve and that is grace. Because if justice is when you get what you deserve and mercy is when you don't get what you deserve, then grace is when you get good things you don't deserve.

Our parable this morning is one of the parables of grace and like all the stories of Jesus it is rich in meaning and there is plenty for us to discuss. Honestly the parable that Jesus tells doesn't seem fair in the least and quite truthfully it isn't because the laborer work a different amount of time yet the all get the same payment. That doesn't seem right to those who worked all day or to us listening and that is perhaps the point of the story itself because buried within the narrative is something that we might overlook in our confusion or outrage on how the workers are paid.

At this point, I need to mention something important. Like all the other parables of Jesus this story is to help us think about and better understand God and God's way. This is not a story about economics or labour practices, but rather a passage to get us thinking about how God's grace can be surprising, unexpected, and even offensive. So I think it is important to focus in on what the workers ask from the owner and what they receive because I think when we are talking about grace we need to pay attention to the fact that grace is something that happens but grace is also the way that someone acts.

Some workers came to the vineyard to work and they negotiated with the landowner for a full days' wage. Keep that point in mind because it is important — the workers asked for what they thought was fair and they got a promise of that from the landowner and then they started to work. After a couple of hours, the landowner hired some workers who were idle to also work for him and listen to what the landowner said, "You also go into the vineyard, and whatever is right I will give you'" (Matthew 20:4 WEB). That line is important because those workers didn't negotiate, they didn't haggle, instead they relied on the landowner to be good to them. The story goes on to say that the landowner hired more workers at noon and three in the afternoon and near the end of the day the landowner found some idle workers and told them to go work also.

Then came the time for everyone to be paid and the ones who came at five o'clock and worked an hour got a full day's wage, as did those who were hired at three and noon. It's not hard to imagine what the workers hired first thing in the morning thought… "Well if those people got a full day's wage for a couple of hours work just imagine what we will receive." And when they got paid they received a full day's wage. Seeing what they were paid compared to what everyone else was paid they were not happy. The parable says that they grumbled against the landowner. They complained that they had worked a full day under the hot sun and got the same wage as the ones who had come at five o'clock and only worked one hour. "That's not fair!" They protested, and you know what? They were right. What everyone was being paid wasn't fair. It was grace.

When the disgruntled workers went to the landowner with their protests, he asked them a very pointed question. "Did I not give you what we agreed on?" The truth is that he did. They asked for a day's wage and they got a day's wage. Remember the other workers, the ones who came later didn't negotiate. They trusted in the landowner's promise to treat them well and my did he ever. He gave them the full day's wage no matter how much they worked. In his reply to the grumbling workers the owner said, "Isn't it lawful for me to do what I want to with what I own?" (Matthew 20:15a WEB). That brings me back to the point that we sometimes overlook about the pay and the workers. Those who began the day negotiated for a full day's wages. They asked for it, the owner agreed to it, and they headed in to work. When the owner found workers later in the day, he offered them the chance to work in the vineyard but there were no negotiations. Later in the morning, at noon, and in the early afternoon he simply said to those he found, "trust me to pay you what is right." The last group, those who had been idle all day, he simply invited to go into the vineyard and made no mention of pay.

Now remember that this story is not instruction from Jesus on how to run a business but insight into the kingdom of God and the way God acts and calls us to live in the world. This is a story that confronts us with the reality of grace and that is why I drew our attention to how the workers approached the landowner because while all the workers receive the same wage the truth is that the ones who rely on the goodness of the landowner are the ones who are truly blessed. They are treated with grace but the ones who negotiate, who bargain on how much they will do for how much reward, get exactly what they ask for. When we take a step back from the parable the truth is that everyone walks away with enough money to provide for themselves and their family. The ones hired at five don't go home with not enough but plenty — as do the ones hired first thing in the morning.

That is a powerful and perhaps disturbing reminder that grace isn't fair because remember earlier I said that that grace is when we get something good that we don't deserve. Grace is also a gift we need to be open to receiving. So if we negotiate with God, if we bargain, then we may get what we ask for but we will never be open to receiving more and experiencing what it means to trust and hope in God's goodness. Don't bargain with God. Don't negotiate for something because you might only get what you ask for. Instead, simply rely on God. If you have a need pray to God and say what the problem is and what you need but always leave God's answer to God's grace. When we rely on God who loves us, wants the best for us, and who has the means and ability to provide a bounty of gifts to help us grow and live then we discover that grace is more wonderful more amazing and more precious than we ever imagined. Through grace, we receive not what we earn deserve or even expect but what God wants for us because of God's love for each and every one of us.

That, my friends, is something we need to understand about the kingdom of heaven. As we work as God's people, as we labor in the vineyard, we know what we have been promised. We receive grace and mercy because that is what God has offered to us. Yet when we see others receiving the same rewards, especially if we do not think they deserve those blessings, we can start to resent them and grumble about it not being fair, that they have not earned those things. Truthfully, they haven't. The truth is, neither have we because God's grace and love are not dependent on us and our efforts, labor, and actions. We don't deserve or earn those things because we are good workers, pious people, or even because we attend church. They are ours because God wants us to have them in our lives. They are ours because of the generosity of God. They are ours because of God's great love and if we understand that then really what right do we have to grumble or complain when God shows that same generosity to others?

When we are speaking about God and God's way, we need to set aside our ideas of what is right and what is fair and understand how God views fairness and righteousness. God wants all people to be blessed and know the gifts that the Spirit brings. The invitation to be a part of God's people and receive forgiveness and salvation are not about us being good enough but rather us accepting those gifts from God. The kingdom of heaven is like a landowner who calls us to work in the vineyard and asks us to trust that we will be treated well. Our reward and our place among God's people, is based not on how long we have answered the call or the results of our labours, but on God's love for each and every one of us.

Amen.

Proper 21 (26)
Matthew 21:23-32

Why Believe In Jesus?

"By what authority do you do these things? Who gave you this authority?" (Matthew 21:23 WEB). The religious leaders of the day confronted Jesus and demanded he prove himself to them. They did that because those leaders believed they had the right and the sacred responsibility to preach and teach about God. That is why they were attacking Jesus. We might assume this was just one more conflict between the religious establishment of the day and Jesus. The truth is, the question about the authority of Jesus isn't confined to the past. People today want to know why they should believe in Jesus. They want to know why they should care about Jesus of Nazareth and what Christianity teaches about him.

Before I go any further, I want to draw a distinction. There is nothing wrong with asking when you are looking for an answer. Jesus never shied away from difficult questions and neither should his followers or the church. Wondering about who Jesus is and why he is important can be an honest inquiry from someone who isn't sure, who has doubts, and who is spiritually seeking. Sometimes, though, when people ask about Jesus they don't want an answer. The religious leaders confronting Jesus had already decided they were not going to believe anything he said. That was not doubt but rather rejection. I say that because no argument, no proof, will sway the mind of a person who has already decided. All you can do is point out that they are not listening.

That is why in our lesson, Jesus replied with a question to those challenging him. He asked if John the Baptist was just a man or sent by God. He asked this because the religious authorities despised John's call for them to repent but the crowds respected John and believed he was a prophet. After some frantic discussion among themselves the religious leaders decided the only safe answer they could give was to say they didn't know if John was sent by God or not. That led Jesus to reply with a parable. "A man had two sons...."

When Jesus begins this morning's parable whether we realize it or not we start to think of all the other stories in the Bible of two sons — Cain and Abel, Jacob and Esau, and even the parable of the prodigal son. We expect that there is one son who does as his father asks and the other who doesn't. When Jesus said *a man has two sons* we are looking for the one we should be like and the one whose behavior or whose attitude is a warning to us. That is where Jesus' story takes a sharp turn.

The man who had two sons asked them to go and work in the vineyard and the first son said he wouldn't and the second said he would. Listening to their answers it seems like we should be like the second son and not like the first. Then Jesus told us that the first son who said no to his father later reconsidered and did what he had been asked. However, the second who said yes to doing as his father wanted never went out to the field as he said he would but instead went off and did something else. Who are we supposed to be like? Surely not the son who said yes but then did nothing and surely not like the son who refused to go as asked but then changed his mind — because honestly neither of them are good role models. The proper thing would be to say yes and then actually do what we are asked and since that describes neither of the sons in the parable, we are left wondering what Jesus was getting at as he told his story. Thinking about it we begin to realize that he was not talking about the ideal way to live but something else entirely that tied into what Jesus was trying to get the religious leaders to see.

The religious leaders believed they were righteous and pious people, yet they rejected John who called them to turn back to God and they rejected Jesus because of his message of mercy and grace. Jesus pointed out that they were still refusing to believe even after they saw the truth of what John was saying. That is why Jesus didn't bother getting into an argument with them about his authority but rather drew attention to their closed minds and blindness to what was happening in front of them. Yet, that was not all that Jesus said through his parable.

Jesus was also reminding us that an open mind or an honest question can lead to understanding and faith. For Jesus says that those who heard John's message and believed that means that those who changed their minds and their lives are the ones who will be a part of what God has promised and prepared because remember that the good son in the parable is not the one who says all the right words but ignores what his father wants. The good son is the one who actually does what was asked, even though initially he refused. That doesn't mean that Jesus held this up as the ideal. The ideal is to say yes to God and then follow through but changing our minds and ways and turning back to God is the next best thing. That brings me to a question that arises from the parable.

Which one are you like? Are you the one who has heard the call of God in your life and said you will live as one of God's people and then never followed through? Or are you the one who never had time or interest in God who now believes maybe you should do what you have been asked to do? Are you sometimes one and at other times the other son from the parable?

No matter whether you are a bit of a hypocrite for saying and not doing, or a sinner for refusing God but thinking of doing what is right, or some combination of those things, the truth is that God invites, God asks, and God calls you to change. God calls you to stop just saying and to start doing. He calls you to make sure that your words match your actions and to repent. The call to repentance, the message of the gospel, is for you in your life. Because that is what Jesus teaches and shows in his life. All of us, you and I, need to change, to turn back to God, to be people who focus on what is right and rely on the goodness of God.

The good news of Jesus Christ is that when we do, God will not only forgive us for what we have done wrong but welcome us fully and completely into the promises that God makes to us through the death and resurrection of Jesus. God will forgive and let go of the wrong you have done. Leave the wrong words and choices of the past behind and turn to what is right and good. Know that God will forgive you and give you another chance to start again — even if you have turned back before, even if you have tried and failed, even if you believe that what you have said or done is unforgivable. God calls you to repent and experience grace.

At this point let me be very blunt and direct as to what that means. If your words have not always matched how Jesus calls you to live, if you have intended to do what is right but have not really followed through then you need to change your life, to follow the way God opens for us, and start living differently now and you need to know, to believe, and to trust that when you do that God forgives and renews your life. God is not interested in the mistakes of the past and how we have all failed but rather wants each and every one of us to move forward as better people, as people who understand the depths of God's love for us.

Then, and only then, do we really start to live within the promises of God, experiencing the power of forgiveness, and the wonder of grace, as we discover the way forward and begin the new life that is ours for the taking. We will begin a new life that God offers to us not because we get everything right and do exactly what we are supposed to do but because we turn to God and experience the power and wonder of what God's love does for us this day and all of our days when we repent and allow that love to shape and guide our lives.

This lesson isn't simply about us but about why we believe and trust and follow Jesus. That means when we hear an honest question about Jesus, when a friend or neighbor asks us why we are Christian or why we go to church, it is important for us to try and answer. It doesn't matter if they have never been to church, had a bad experience, or have some serious doubts. What matters is that we tell why we go to church, why we believe in Jesus and the difference all that makes to us so that they might better understand about God and faith and so that in telling others we might be reminded of what God asks from us in the world.

We follow Jesus because we believe he is the one who shows us the face of God. His stories and sayings recorded in the gospels challenge us to recognize God's love for us and to live lives that are filled with forgiveness and hope. Jesus proclaims a way of love and mercy, of compassion and grace. Jesus invites us to break down barriers and to live connected with God and other people and his actions illustrate and give meaning to those words. He refuses to let hypocrisy, selfishness, and evil go unchallenged. His arms are open to the rejected, the wounded, and the lost. Through healing, miracles, and self-sacrifice Jesus shows what mercy and compassion really mean as he demonstrates the power of God's love. Those two things, his words and his actions, make Jesus a great teacher and a powerful prophet of God.

We also believe that his death upon the cross is the means by which God brings forth the resurrection, that through Jesus a new creation is underway. A reordering of our world, our lives, our future, is now possible because Jesus lived, died, and lives again. The cross and empty tomb are the signs that God through Jesus is transforming life itself. The empty cross stands as a reminder that nothing can stop God from reaching into our world and touching our lives with grace, mercy, and forgiveness. Nothing we have done, no power in this world, not even death itself can prevent that from happening. The empty tomb is the promise that we can begin fresh, start new lives, because the power that brought creation into being has begun a new creation, a new life here and now, that we are invited to share in.

That is why as a church we believe in Jesus, that is why as disciples we proclaim his death and resurrection; that is why as Christians we follow his way and work to show grace and hope to the world. I'm not saying that everyone has to accept, believe, and adhere to the words that the church has used to describe those beliefs, or even that we have to be certain about everything that is part of the Christian faith. No, what we need to do is be people with open eyes and hearts who listen to the call of Jesus in our lives and respond. God invites us to come with our questions as well as our answers and live within the power of the Holy Spirit at work in the world.

We are challenged to dare to hope that all those things that we are unsure about can be true. Jesus never asks us to be completely certain but to trust, to believe, and to know that we are welcome this day to enter and be a part of all that God has promised and all that God is doing.

Amen.

The Surprise Of Salvation

It was dusk this time last year when I went to pick my daughter up from her after school program. I had just turned at the traffic light when I heard a siren and saw the red and blue lights in the rear-view mirror. I pulled over and frantically reviewed the last few minutes. I had turned on the green light, I hadn't been speeding, I had signaled on both turns, and hadn't cut anyone off.

My mind was still racing when I rolled down the window for the approaching constable who told me that my headlights weren't on. Within seconds I put the headlights on and the police officer told me to drive carefully. As I slowly pulled out, I was mindful that sometimes we can do lots of things right and still get something important wrong.

The parable from Matthew 22:33-46 follows the parable of the two sons (Matthew 21:23-32) where Jesus warned the religious leaders that those who repent will enter kingdom of heaven before them. While the parable from this lesson is not that familiar, the truth is that the story isn't hard to follow. A man established a vineyard, found some tenants to run it, and then went away. He repeatedly sent servants to collect the rent and the tenants refused to pay. They beat, stoned or killed the servants. Then the landowner sent his son thinking "they will respect my son" (Matthew 21:37 WEB) but the tenants didn't and they attacked and killed him as well. Jesus asked the listeners what they thought the landowner would do when he finally came to reclaim his vineyard.

But, before we get to the answer about what the landowner would do, I want to talk about a few of the confusing things that happen in the parable. The first is the behavior of the tenants. They treated the servants of the landowner badly when the servants came to collect what was owed to their master. They resorted to violence. That honestly makes no sense because there seems to be no reason for them to go to such extremes. After all, they didn't grumble that the rent was too high or that they couldn't make ends meet but rather acted as if they owed the landowner nothing. That, I think, points to why the message of the servants coming to collect the rent was so offensive to the tenants. The tenants believed that the vineyard was theirs to do with as they would. They thought that what they had been allowed to use under certain conditions was actually theirs to do with as they pleased and that no one had the right to demand anything from them and they would do anything to preserve that lie — even resorting to violence.

Now like all the other parables Jesus told, this story of tenants and vineyards was not about landowners and farmers but about God's will and way. The story points to the uncomfortable truth that we sometimes don't like what God says to us in our lives. We eagerly listen to the message of God's love and grace, but when the conversation shifts to God's expectations and the call to repent from the evil we are doing, we squirm in our seats, we no longer want to listen, and maybe we protest that judgment has nothing to do with us and the way we are living.

After all, we prefer being told that we're great the way we are instead of being told that we need to turn away from sin and do better. We like hearing how we are loved, not that we have to love the people we have difficulty with in life. We want messages about what God gives rather than messages about what God asks and the call to repent, to change, or to understand. God's way is hardest for us to hear when we think are already doing everything right and there is no need for us to change in any way. That brings us to the reaction of the tenants in the parable when the son was sent. They saw the son and said to each other "This is the heir. Come, let's kill him and seize his inheritance" (Matthew 21:38b WEB). When you think about that, it makes absolutely no sense at all. The vineyard didn't belong to them and it was the landowner's to do with as he pleased. If they killed the heir, they still had to deal with the landowner and his rage.

At this point in the story, I need to mention something that is important. There is nothing in the parable to suggest that the tenants were bad farmers or destroying the vineyard. The landowner didn't send the servants or the son to drive them from the land or demand they become anything other than the farmers they already were. As far as we know, the tenants were producing a crop and doing things right but, and this is the confusing thing, they seemed to have the idea that the vineyard should belong to them and they could have it if they could just stop the landowner from sending servants or family to collect the rent.

The uncomfortable truth is that sometimes we think we are doing everything right and we are still in the wrong. That's what struck me when the constable pulled me over that night when my headlights were off in the car. I was doing so many things just like I was supposed to, following the law, but there was something I was missing and that was a problem and that brings us to the reality of salvation. We'd like to think that we're good enough as we are or that if we just a bit did more than we would have everything we want or need. We'd like to believe that there is something we can do, we can make ourselves good enough, to earn or deserve heaven and all of God's promises but we can't earn salvation and we don't deserve the grace of God any more than the tenants can inherit the vineyard. The truth is that heaven, salvation, and the promises of God are gifts of God and only come to us because of who God is and what God chooses to do.

All of that leads us to the last big surprise of the reading and actually isn't in the parable itself. It comes at the very end when Jesus asked those who were listening what the landowner would do to the tenants after they killed his son. The religious leaders had no hesitation and said that the landowner would come with a vengeance and punish them, then cast them out and lease the vineyard to other tenants. Jesus seemed to agree with them as he talked about stones being rejected and how that stone would be broken and crush everyone. Except, this was a parable of Jesus and Jesus was still talking to the Pharisees and religious leaders about the kingdom of God, the promised time and place of God, and how that would come to the people. That turns everything we assume upside down.

When Jesus asked what the landowner would do to the occupiers of the vineyard who had forgotten that they did not own the land but simply rented it, would react to the killing of the messengers and the murder of his son, the Pharisees gave the answer we would expect if we were talking about an earthly landowner and tenants. The landowner would deal with them harshly for abusing his servants and killing his heir, his son. The response we expect would be full of fury and violence.

Yet we actually know what happened to the people who killed the son of God, don't we? We know what God the Father did when Jesus the Son was broken on the cross and died because the people could not accept his words or message. God chose to forgive and chose not to condemn the world but through the death of Jesus ensured the salvation of the world. The truth is that when Jesus was broken on the cross, when he became the stone rejected by the builders because he was not what they were looking for, then God was able to enter into our lives and our world to bring healing and new life. For God knows our unworthiness and loves us anyway. God understands our weakness and sin yet offers us a way to experience forgiveness and grace.

There is a warning in our parable that we need to hear. Jesus is telling us that we need to stop deluding ourselves that what we have and enjoy is actually ours and if we just get rid of God in some way then we can have even more. It isn't an easy message to hear. That is why the lesson ended with the religious leaders of the day realizing that Jesus was talking about them and they were furious because they didn't think they needed to repent of anything for any reason and like the tenants in the parable they plotted to kill the son and silence his message. But before we close our Bibles and file this parable away as another story where Jesus offended some self-righteous and uptight people let's be a bit humble.

Let's admit we got the answer to the question Jesus asked about what the landowner would do with the tenants wrong —

despite the fact that we actually spent our whole time singing, praying, and trying to live in and by God's grace and mercy as the church. In humility, we have to go back to the passage and realize that we can't simply point our finger at somebody else and say, "they are wrong because they are like the tenants." We understand ourselves as the people who inherit the promises of God, the people who bear witness to the love of God, and the ones through whom God is working, and that actually can make us assume we are owed the kingdom of heaven. That makes us more like the tenants than we would like to admit.

As well as that warning, I think the parable also offers us a deeper insight into the gospel. When we do not feel worthy, don't feel that we deserve God's grace and love, mercy and blessings, and that is when we are actually open to knowing and experiencing salvation in our lives. God comes into our world, where prophets have been stoned and ignored, and chooses not to destroy but to redeem.

Salvation, the promise of new life now and eternal life to come, has never been about what we can do and what we get but about what God can do and what God gives. In the cross of Jesus, we see for ourselves the presence and power of God shown not in anger and vengeance but in forgiveness and grace and that is the message that we as followers of Jesus are called to proclaim and embody.

We are to show people the reality of who God is through the words we speak and the actions we take. We are to tell them that there is salvation and hope even if they have always rejected God. No matter what they have done, the good news of Jesus Christ is that God chooses to forgive, chooses to embrace, and chooses to transform the cross from a symbol of pain and suffering into a beacon of hope and renewal.

The cross is an invitation for us to change, to become new people and to live within the gifts of God and know the blessings and reality of what God intends for us and the world. To understand that while we are getting some of the things we are meant to do right, the truth is that some of our lives, or sometimes a fundamental part of our lives, that needs to be transformed. We can have that happen because each of us, you and I, are welcome to come to that cross and experience for ourselves the new life and new hope that is ours because God answers our world, answers our sin, and answers our lives with grace and love.

Amen.

Proper 23 (28)
Matthew 22:1-14

Dealing With The Invitation

The parable of the wedding from Matthew 22:1-14 is not a story that most of us know that well. Part of that is because the story is not a pleasant one to hear and part of that is because the meaning isn't obvious. Yet the truth is that like the other stories of Jesus this is not a difficult story to follow. There was a king who gave a banquet for his son and invited a number of guests to the celebration. The guests, though, decided not to go to the feast. Some went home, others to work, and still others got angry and beat the messengers who had come to invite them.

The way the invited guests acted was rude at best and down-right insulting and offensive at worst. When the king invited them to know the bounty of his generosity the potential guests responded with indifference, insult, and anger. That was a strange way to give thanks for an invitation to share in someone else's wealth and if this wasn't a parable of Jesus we could probably shrug or shake our heads at how foolish some people are. Yet this is a story Jesus used to teach about God and God's way so we need to pay attention to what Jesus said about the guests and their reaction to the invitation to the wedding feast.

The first group invited to the wedding went home instead of to the feast. They looked to what they had instead of what had been offered to them. The truth is that sometimes we don't look beyond our leisure activities, the things we eat and drink, and the pleasures we find in life. We assume that what we have is all that we need to have in life or perhaps more disturbingly all that we can have.

I think it is important to be honest and admit that we all have things in life that are wonderful and that we are grateful for. We have health, friends, family, and things that give us delight and joy in life. This parable wasn't saying that those things are bad or that we shouldn't like them or appreciate them. The fact is that in our parable the king offered the guests more than what they already had and they simply ignored the invitation and went home.

God has blessed us, each of us, with many good things but the reality is that there is more that God offers and invites us to know and experience in life. For what we have now in our lives is not the best of what God offers or wants us to have. The invitation, the welcome of the cross, is to know grace and love, peace and hope and to experience more, much more, than we already know. So, like the first group of guests we can hear that invitation and go home, or we can come and experience the bounty and blessings that are being offered to us.

The second group of people chose to go to work. They heard the invitation and went to their labors and efforts. We know there were things that need to be done in life and we all have families to provide for and tasks that need to be completed. Work, whether paid work like an occupation or unpaid work like caring for a family or raising children, is something that gives us meaning and purpose in life and can be fulfilling and I'm not suggesting that work is a bad thing. I honestly believe that work, what we can create and do with our bodies and minds, can be a gift from God just like the other good things in life but, and this is important, work is not the purpose and goal of our lives. We are not created to work but rather work is one of the things we can do. In our parable the guests who chose to go to work decided to focus on what they knew they could do instead of turning to and trusting in the generosity of the invitation they had received.

Honestly, it isn't easy to trust in grace. The invitation of the gospel, the call of Jesus Christ is at its heart an invitation for us to trust in the goodness of God. We can't earn the mercy and forgiveness God offers. We can't work to make the love and grace God gives. All of those things are gifts and they come not because of what we do but because of who God is and what God chooses to do. It is tempting to trust not in grace but in the work of our own hands but the reality is that just like believing what we have is all that we can ever have, thinking that if we don't work for it we can't have it also shuts us off from receiving what God offers. For in this parable those who go to work miss out on what the king offers to them at the banquet.

That leads us to the last group of people who responded by beating the messengers and I'll admit this is a confusing response. After all they were being invited to a feast, a banquet, a celebration, so why would they respond with anger and violence? I could also ask why you and I sometimes get upset when we hear of someone else's good fortune or why the invitation of the gospel, to know God's love and grace sometimes brings such an angry response from people. It could be that we don't want others to rejoice when we are hurting or in pain or in sorrow. It may be that we feel that a celebration for someone else has somehow diminished our lives. It might be that we react be pushing away when we fear, we worry, we think that the invitation somehow mocks us, ignores us, or will hurt us. Sometimes I think a negative response is a human reaction that we simply will never completely understand.

In our parable, the king reacted when he heard that the invited guests ignored the invitation and I think we need to be careful and understand as always that in the parables Jesus told that he was making a point we need to hear. The king reacted to the violence by sending in his troops and delivering what would have been seen at the time as justice. I know hearing of the violence of the king's troops is disturbing to our ears but the truth is that none of us are that comfortable hearing about judgment.

Yet Jesus was never shy about teaching that there is judgment and there are consequences in life and notice that the king didn't send the troops to seize the guests and force them to go to the banquet. No, the king left those who went home in their homes and left those who went to work at their work. They weren't punished for rejecting the invitation but they were left with the limited lives and empty efforts that they had always known; but for those who broke the law, who reacted with violence then they experienced punishment and destruction. They rejected the king's invitation by causing harm and the king could not and would not tolerate that.

God invites each and every one of us to know the salvation and new life that is ours through Jesus Christ and if we choose to ignore that invitation then God lets us. If we trust simply in what we have or what we can do then God lets us because God is not a tyrant who forces us to believe or act as a follower of Jesus but, and this is important, just because God lets us make our own choices does not mean there are no consequences or judgment from God. If you turn away from God you will not receive the salvation that God offers. You will not know the blessings and possibilities that God opens up for you. If you focus your life on yourself then God will not punish you or destroy you but you will never live up to the potential God created you for and your life will be limited not to what God offers but to yourself. For God will not force you to repentance but will leave you, I think with regret and sorrow, to your choice.

Yet if you reject God and choose a path of violence and harm then you will discover that the way you have chosen is one that will bring violence and harm into your own life. There are consequences, there is judgment, and justice is not kind to those who break the laws set out by God. When you refuse to appeal to mercy and grace, and if that was all to the parable, then this story would be a parable of judgment, a stark reminder that we need to heed the call, the invitation, that God makes to us through the life, death, and resurrection of Jesus Christ. Yet there is more to the story.

The king invited new guests to the feast. He sent the servants out far and wide and filled the hall with guests and interestingly the text tells us that both good and bad were brought to the banquet. While that small detail may seem unimportant, I think that it is at the heart of the parable. Everyone was invited. We don't know if the original guests were good and bad although I think it is probably safe to say they were a mixture of both given their reaction to the invitation. Yet here we are told explicitly that the new guests were both good and bad (Matthew 22:10). That meant that the invitation offered by the king wasn't just for the holy and virtuous, although they were certainly invited too, but also to those who hadn't lived the best lives, who had fallen and been broken by life. Those who had made bad choices, given into temptation, or who had done wrong. They were there at the feast, enjoying the bounty and generosity of the king that is how we understand the gospel. The invitation to know the blessings and grace of God isn't simply from those who are good, those who are holy, but for all people regardless of how we have lived until this point in our lives. There is blessing and hope, there is forgiveness and new life for us all through the grace and love of God. Yet Jesus still isn't done with the story.

The king noticed a wedding guest who wasn't dressed for a wedding and got angry and cast him out. We get a usual ending in the parables of judgment from Matthew about weeping and gnashing of teeth in the darkness. The truth is that this unpleasant ending is a reminder that while we are all invited there is an expectation that we actually respond to the invitation. It is not enough to just show up but it is essential that the invitation change you and how you answer. I think before we start to worry about whether we are worthy in our response to God's invitation to Jesus, and if it is good enough, we need to remember that in the parable the king wasn't upset that the wedding guest didn't have on fancy enough clothes or that the style was wrong but that the guest showed up dressed for something other than a wedding. In other words, the guest wasn't there to celebrate the reason the king invited him.

The invitation we all receive through Jesus Christ is an invitation to know and experience the blessings and bounty of what God wishes to give to us in life. The invitation is to be saved, to be loved, to know peace and mercy and grace in our lives, and all of that is what God wants to give to us and offers to us through Jesus. All we need to do to receive those things is to answer. We need to open our hearts to accept what God gives and allow those things that invitation to change who we are even as we begin to experience and know the deeper blessings and life that are ours through the life, the death, and the resurrection of Jesus Christ.

Amen.

A Challenging Answer

"Is it lawful to pay taxes or not?" No one likes to pay taxes and we can quibble about whether the money is being used responsibly or not but the fact is that we can see what our taxes provide. Among other things our taxes pay for the roads that we drive on each day, the schools our children attend, the parks we enjoy, and the police and fire services that are there when we need them. The question in our gospel lesson of whether it is lawful to pay taxes seems straightforward — except that it's not for two reasons.

The first is that the people where Jesus lived were a conquered people. The people surrounding Jesus were living in an occupied land and the taxes they paid to Caesar or the emperor went to Rome. The money went out of their country to another and didn't provide them with any real benefits. If fact, part of the money they had to provide in taxes went to pay for the soldiers who enforced the will of the emperor and some of the money lined the pockets of corrupt and greedy officials. The people got nothing for their taxes except grief and more taxes. While the Roman governor required the money from the conquered land there was no one who paid the tax who thought it was right or fair.

The second reason the question is complicated is that the people asking Jesus weren't wondering about the law of the land. Remember before they asked their question there was that long preamble about how Jesus's taught God's way (Matthew 22:16). What the questioners wanted to know was not whether taxes were required but whether good, moral, God fearing people should pay taxes to the emperor. The Pharisees and Herodians publicly asked Jesus if it was faithful, something a good person did, something lawful under the commandments of God, to pay taxes to an evil empire that rejected God and brought suffering to so many and the answer seems obvious — we shouldn't support such a thing with our money and in fact the faithful response is to resist such oppression and evil with all our might.

Yet, this is a trick question. We know that because the reading begins by telling us that some Pharisees were trying to trap Jesus with a question. What we might have missed was that there were also some Herodians in that group and like the name suggests those people were followers of Herod, who ruled as a puppet of the Roman occupiers. That made this not merely a trick question but a dangerous question. While on the surface the question seems like an honest inquiry — how do we reconcile faith and what the world asks of us — the question was actually an attempt to destroy the reputation and ministry of Jesus.

If Jesus said no to paying taxes, then the Herodians would rush off to tell the Romans and Jesus would be arrested and if Jesus said yes, then the Pharisees would tell the people Jesus was in league with the Romans. So there seems to be no answer and honestly there isn't but Jesus answered them anyway.

He asked one of the questioners to show him a coin used to pay the taxes and tell him whose picture was on it and what their title was. That was the point where the plan to trap Jesus started to come apart because the Pharisees had to answer that the coin had the picture of the emperor on it. Roman coins all have pictures of the emperor on them and underneath the picture are inscriptions. Those inscriptions state that the emperor is divine, a god to be worshiped. Remember the ten commandments told the people not to have idols in their homes and yet the religious people questioning Jesus were carrying pictures of a Roman god.

When Jesus asked for a coin he was showing that the questioners had given in to pressures in the world and were breaking religious laws in doing so. That led to the words he said: "Give therefore to Caesar the things that are Caesar's, and to God the things that are God's" (Matthew 22:21 WEB). This was a response that amazed everyone because it answered the question and made sense to both the crowds and the Romans.

The Romans heard Jesus say that people should pay taxes and they had no argument with that. The crowds heard Jesus say they were to give to the Romans what belonged to them and they couldn't really dispute that. If the coin was Roman and the Romans wanted it back, then you should give it to them. The answer was simple and straightforward but the truth is that Jesus was saying something a bit more complicated in his answer. He didn't just say give to the emperor what belonged to the emperor he also said give to God what belongs to God. While sometimes the verse has been taken to mean pay your taxes the truth is that was not the question that Jesus answered.

The questioners showed Jesus a Roman coin, minted by the Romans, distributed by the Romans, and wondered if the Romans had any claim on it. Jesus dismissed the question of who deserved it. If it was a Roman coin, why shouldn't the Roman emperor have it back? At this point we realize that Jesus wasn't answering about whether it was lawful or right to pay taxes. After all, if you were a person living in the land in those days you really didn't have any choice because the money was collected at the point of a sword. The tribute coin may have had an idol on it but the Romans wouldn't accept anything else so you really had no choice. No, the real question Jesus was focusing us on was what was right, true, and good in our lives. How are we to live as God's people in the world? The real point Jesus wanted us to hear, the message we need to understand is, "Give to God what belongs to God" and think about that part of the passage for a moment.

What belongs to God? What do we owe God? How do we give to God what belongs to God? Thinking about those questions we realize that Jesus' answer is not simply to accept what is happening in the world and do whatever we are told but that our lives within the world are always and at every moment to be lived out in faith. God gives us everything we have: our lives, grace, mercy, peace, hope, and unending love, and we in turn owe it to God to live in answer to those gifts. With those two phrases put together Jesus is saying that it was fine to live in a society with laws and things like taxes. They are part of life on earth. You live among people with different values, beliefs, and practices and there are demands on you from them but, and this is what is important, the fact is that our first obligation, our priority is on answering God in our lives. We are to be good citizens but our most important quality is to be good people of faith.

I want to be clear I'm not simply talking about us being good citizens in the land in that we reside. We are children of God, living in the world God created for us and we are called to be part of God's kingdom. There is a difference between being a good citizen of a nation and being part of God's kingdom because being a good, right, moral person involves something deeper, more foundational about how we live our lives than simply not breaking laws or avoiding wrong. Good citizens follow the laws. God's people do God's work.

I know that may be a distinction blurred in our minds so let me put it this way: someone does not become your friend because they don't hurt you, don't lie to you, and don't steal from you. That person is being lawful, doing what is required of them under the laws of this land but they don't become your friend, someone close to you, by doing only that. No, someone becomes a friend because they help you, they tell you the truth, and they give of themselves to you. That is how you become a friend. In the world God calls us to do well. To give back to God what God has given to us that requires more of us than simply following laws.

Thankfully for us most of the time the laws of the land and God's law line up. I have no problem telling you to pay your taxes because I know how those taxes help people and provide services that we all need, but there are times that the demands of this world and the call of God are at odds. When we are asked to tolerate things that are unjust and wrong. When we are told to be quiet when we call for justice and fairness and when our neighbors push for violence rather than reconciliation. When the demands of the world lead away from God. At those times our priority, our decision, must be to answer God and follow Christ in our lives for that is what it means to give back to God what God has given us.

God has given us life, grace, mercy, and opportunity and we are to live faithfully in community with others and work to build a better world. We are to help others not because they earn it or deserve it but because we are acting as God has acted toward us in Jesus. We are to use what we have, what we have been given, to promote and encourage what is good and what is beautiful. We are to reconcile and build cooperation especially when we become divided. We are to seek what God intends and be a part of what God is doing in the world.

All of that means there is a real challenge in Jesus' words because we are God's people, called to follow in the way Jesus leads us and to be good, moral, and compassionate people, then that requires us to *be* more and *do* more than simply being lawful. Yes, obeying the just laws of our land is a start but God calls us to something more profound and more transformative. We are to be lights shining in the darkness, showing the way for people to live and the beauty that God has placed in everything. We are to be the salt of the earth. That means we are to enrich the joys of the world and purify the wrongs around us. We are to be the living embodiment of grace and compassion, hope and peace. When the people around us see our lives, see our actions, hear our words they can see the gospel message at work.

All of that happens when we answer God with our lives. All of that happens when we live in faith, trusting in the salvation of the cross and the new life of the resurrection. It happens when we choose to let love guide our actions and allow grace to motivate our actions. It happens when we open our hearts and allow the Holy Spirit to move within us. It happens when we open our hands and let grace and gratitude guide our actions. It happens when we come together in order to build a land of justice and hope, of joy and peace, and when we give back to God what God has given to us.

God through Jesus gives us forgiveness and mercy, a new life here and eternal life to come. God asks that we answer that gift, acknowledge that opportunity, by living our lives in response. He asks that we answer by being people who are all the things the questioners spoke of before they questioned Jesus — by being sincere and by teaching in word and example the way of God and the truth of grace.

Amen.

The Heart Of Faith

"What is the greatest commandment?" This is like the question from a bit earlier in the gospel about paying taxes that seems like an honest question. After all shouldn't we all be aware of the most important thing for us to do as people of faith? Shouldn't we focus on what is important and place less emphasis on the things that aren't? The truth is, that is actually the problem with the question. It asks us to pick and choose among the things God says, discarding some while paying attention to others.

It's like asking someone what the most important traffic law to obey is. There really is no answer. All the laws are important. Stopping at stop signs keeps you from having accidents. So does driving on the proper side of the road. You can't just arbitrarily pick one and say that law is important and the others are not. The laws fit together to let us drive and walk around traffic in safety. God's commandments and laws are given so that we understand what God wants and we do things that are faithful as we live our lives. To pick one above the others is really missing the point of why God asks those things from us.

They are all important in their own way and fit together to lead and guide us to a better life. God's law was given to us so that we can live in the way God intends. Some of them tell us what not to do, like the commandments to not kill, steal, or lie. Others talk about what we need to do like keep a sabbath and honor our family commitment. The Pharisee wanted Jesus to say that one was best. He wanted Jesus to state which law was better than the other laws. That misses the point of why we have laws. You can't pick a law and say it is better than any other law. They're all important for us to know and follow in order to have a right relationship with God and each other. That is actually what Jesus answered — for Jesus answered that the most important commandment is love.

Jesus said, "'You shall love the Lord your God with all your heart, with all your soul, and with all your mind.' This is the first and greatest commandment. A second likewise is this, 'You shall love your neighbor as yourself'" (Matthew 22:47-48 WEB). Growing up I always thought that it was a strange answer to the question of what is the greatest commandment because Jesus didn't give one answer, he actually gave two: Love God — love your neighbor. Those are the two greatest commandments. Yet the truth is that we can't have one without the other. We need the two of them to express and shape the other; that is pretty much how the law works. Not simply showing us specifics that God wants but show us the life God calls us to live as people of faith. That actually helps us know what Jesus was doing with his answer because instead of picking the most important law, Jesus answered about what was the most important thing for us to do — loving God and loving our neighbor.

In answering this way, Jesus shifts us from thinking about what part of the scriptures is more important to thinking about what is behind all the things God asks. Jesus moves us from wondering about what *I* should do to thinking about how *we* are to live as followers of Jesus. All of that is why Jesus' answer doesn't talk about the importance of the commandments and rules God gives to us but gets us thinking about why God gives us those things. Why does God give us commandments and rules? What is behind everything that God asks? Jesus very clearly answered that behind everything God asks of us, and the way for us to do those things, is love.

Drawn from verses in the book of Deuteronomy and Leviticus the dual command to love God and neighbor would also have been very familiar to the people of Jesus' time so few if any would have been surprised when Jesus highlighted these commandments as crucial. Deuteronomy 6:5 calls the people to love God and Leviticus 19:18 tells us to love our neighbors as ourselves. Jesus' specific response was taken from scriptures that his listeners would know and would agree were essential parts of faith. As Jesus answered the question, he got to the heart of the matter and showed us that the reason for things like the ten commandments is to help us to love God and love our neighbor.

Jesus didn't merely use these words to teach others — they were in fact the basis for the life that he lived. Love for God and for neighbor can been seen in things Jesus did, the stories he told, and the person he was. Indeed the new commandment that Jesus gave in the upper room was to encourage the disciples to love, as they had been commanded, using him as an example — "Love one another even as I have loved you" (John 15:12b WEB).

We are told as people of faith to love God and love our neighbor. Jesus said that the law and the prophets come from these commands and again that shows us what Jesus was doing with his answer. He was reinforcing that the law is not a separate group of instructions that you can pick and choose but rather something that all comes, flows, from what God asks of us. At this point I think it is important to note that what Jesus quoted were *commands* not suggestions or ideas to consider. These were demands from God. *Love me, love your neighbor*, and spoken like that they may seem like a strange command for God to make to us. How can we order someone to have affection for us? How can we require a feeling or emotion?

The truth is that when the Bible speaks about love it doesn't start and stop with the feeling as we often do. The biblical understanding of love has to do with commitment and action. When we are commanded to love we are being directed to act in a certain way. We are asked to push past our preferences, experiences, and feelings and use these as our basis for our words and our deeds as the vision and perspective of God.

We are commanded to love our neighbors as ourselves. We are commanded to treat others with as much patience, understanding, and dedication as we treat ourselves. Actually, depending on how you want to read the Greek it can also read "love your neighbor as your own kin" but it really doesn't matter because the intention is the same. We are commanded to look at the stranger, the enemy, the people who frighten us, who bother us, who test our patience, who bore us — we are commanded to look at them and see someone that God loves. We are to see someone we are called to cherish in the same way that God does.

We are challenged in the commandment to see those around us as beloved children of God. We are challenged to look at the people on the streets as precious and important to the God who made everyone. To recognize the person sitting beside us, even though they look different, believe different things, or have ideas we don't share, to see those people as sisters and brothers. To understand that the person who has hurt us, who makes us angry, who says or does things to annoy us, to understand that is the person whom Jesus Christ came and died for on the cross.

That means we are to feed them when they are hungry. Clothe them when they are cold. Visit them when they are lonely. Comfort them when they despair. Share with them the good news of Jesus Christ whenever and however we can. Live a life that expresses, shows, and shares the love of God with them. We are commanded to love our neighbors, care for them, and accept them in a way greater than our human acceptance and caring. Knowing God and understanding Jesus as our role model, we are to see the world with God's eyes and reach out with Christ's compassion. That brings us back to the first part of the greatest commandment that fits hand in hand with the second.

We are commanded to love God. Again, this is not about feeling a certain way about God but is about being committed to God and working to building a relationship with God. Spending time in prayer, searching with our minds to understand what God wishes us to know, feeling with our hearts the passion that God has for us is in that commitment. Knowing in our souls a truth that many times cannot be explained but can always be experienced is also a part of that commitment.

The two greatest commandments go together and really can't be separated. By loving God we come to see our neighbor in a different way. Loving our neighbor enlarges our world as we connect to others. By loving God our possibilities and potential are no longer limited or restricted. By loving our neighbor we act as God's hands and feet and voices. Loving God and our neighbor we live as we were created to live — with God and with each other and in doing those things our uncertain world becomes a place of certainty even when we don't know what tomorrow will bring. Our confusing world becomes straightforward even though we may still not know everything. Our lives become grounded in something more than ourselves and our abilities. Our lives grow because we build them with direction from the author of life and the architect of creation. Our world changes as we bring love into lives that need to experience compassion and mercy.

All of that happens with each time we give to another, with each word we speak in faith, with each moment we consider a scripture, with each opportunity we take to pray, and with each action that brightens a life. With our care of those around us and in our service to God we become the people God calls us to be and we help create the world God desires for us for we are commanded to love God and love our neighbor. We are called to be individuals who push the boundaries of what we can do. We are commanded to think of more than ourselves and become people of grace in the world for there is no doubt in scripture that love is the basis of God's relationship with us and God wants love to be the foundation of how we treat one another and that is therefore the greatest commandment — Love God and love your neighbor.

All of that is why Jesus spoke so much about love. That is why he showed compassion and mercy. That is why he was patient with honest inquirers and welcoming of the children who came to him. That is why he died on the cross — in an effort to show us how powerful and crucial God's love is for our world and for our lives. Jesus came among us to share God's love, to show God's love, and to call us to live God's love. For the greatest commandment Jesus gave is not merely the response to a trick question but rather the heart of the Christian message. Jesus calls us to recognize that love is the foundation for faithful living.

Love doesn't replace the commandments but rather gives them life. We follow the Ten Commandments not because we don't want God to punish us but so that we can love God and love our neighbor. We follow the law that God has set out for us, not so that we can be perfect in our actions but so that we can be directed and guided to be loving people. Love is the basis of what God has called us to be as people of faith. When we love, we know God and we share the gospel of Christ with the world.

Amen.

Blessed Are You

Broken hearted — filled with doubt. No one ever wants to feel that way because when you're consumed by grief the world is gray and painful and when you are filled with doubt it consumes your life and hope becomes distant and unreal. All we want is for those times to end.

Persecuted — bullied. No one ever wants to be in those situations because when you are persecuted or bullied you live in fear and terror overtakes your every thought and action. During those times we feel alone, we feel desperate, we despair. All we want is for life to be different and into those situations, into those times, Jesus delivers a surprising promise.

The beginning of the fifth chapter of Matthew is sometimes known as the Beatitudes. The statements are called that because of the Latin translation (*beati*) of the Greek word (*makarioi*) that Jesus used to start each of the familiar sayings. For us the usual English translation for the Greek is "blessed" although some of the more modern versions use the word "happy" at the start of the sayings. The verses are familiar to many of us because, if you grew up in the church, the start to the Sermon on the Mount was often taught as memory verses that earned you a gold star beside your name in Sunday school. If you were able to recite them correctly and because they were so familiar, you were rewarded. I think we have to be so careful when we listen to these teachings from Jesus because it is really tempting to consider them instructions on how to please God and get a reward. Be merciful, be pure in heart, be meek, be a peacemaker, and you'll get good things from God. In fact, Martin Luther, the great reformer, in his commentary on the beatitudes actually denounced the preachers who were making the beatitudes into instructions on how to get God to bless you rather than proclaiming the words to be an incredible promise of God's grace.

That is why I started this sermon by talking about the terrible situations we find ourselves in because no one wants to be without faith or spiritually poor. No one wants to be in mourning, no one wants to be hungry and thirsting for justice, no one wants to be persecuted for any reason. Yet the truth is that at times we find ourselves there. Despite our best intentions, our best efforts, we find ourselves brokenhearted, wracked with doubt, persecuted, and bullied and this is where we come into the good news Jesus proclaimed. Into those deplorable times when we feel abandoned, afraid, and broken Jesus said these surprising words. You will be blessed. God will not leave you where you are. God will touch your life with grace, with something unexpected and wonderful. You will be blessed. Let me play with the phrasing for a moment because sometimes the familiar beautiful words we learned so many years ago get in the way of us hearing what Jesus is saying.

> *You will be blessed by God when you have no faith, when you struggle to believe, because God will give you the kingdom of heaven.*
>
> *You will be blessed by God when you are broken hearted, when your soul aches and grief overwhelms you, because God will hold you in those times.*
>
> *You will be blessed by God when you cry out for justice, when you need righteousness, because God will bring those things to you.*
>
> *You will be blessed by God when people mock you, despise you, hate you for being a disciple of the Savior because you will be just like one of the prophets in the Bible.*

When the situation is terrible and you cannot do anything about it then God, and God alone, is the one who makes it different. God is the one who comes to those suffering, broken, despairing, and turns the world upside down for them. God is the one who can transform what *is* into what *can be*. God is the one who can make life from death, joy from sorrow, and peace from chaos. I think there is something important we need to realize about these surprising words of grace. Jesus never limits them. Jesus never says blessed are you when through no fault of your own and despite your best efforts this bad thing happens. Jesus never says blessed are you if you are good and holy and difficult times are taking place in your lives.

No, Jesus just said blessed are those who mourn, who are persecuted, who hunger and thirst for righteousness, who are poor in spirit. The promise is the same whether we have some responsibility for what is happening, whether we are blameless, or some combination of the two. The promise is the same if the situation is because of what we have done, what someone else has done, or simply happened because ultimately the message is not about whether we deserve grace but about God. The message in these words of Jesus, these surprising promises are about God's goodness, God's unwillingness to leave us lost, broken, and alone. We are blessed because God loves us and acts to bless us. The reason we are in pain or in sorrow isn't what is important. The responsibility, the guilt, the shame we might bear is not what is important. What is important, what brings about the change, what makes the difference is God's grace.

That's the message of the gospel, the good news that Jesus shared with the people. And as Jesus began to teach the crowd, to teach us about God and God's kingdom in the sermon on the mount, Jesus spoke about the human condition, the places we find ourselves in life, and God's response to us. That's why these words are not instructions about how to live but rather promises of how God will meet us in our grief, our doubts, our isolation, and despair. That's why these words are not limited or restricted to whether we are guilty or innocent, responsible or blameless. That is simple enough to see in the Beatitudes I have gone through. The words are clear in the promise and in the hope that in the worst of life God comes to us with grace, with a new change and a fresh start, an unexpected blessing. They stand as a clear if not surprising statement on how God can change, transform, and make new. They are about how God's grace will meet us in the worst of life and bring what we need.

The truth is that we haven't made the whole way through the beatitudes and it gets a bit more complicated when we talk about the blessings that Jesus proclaimed for the ways we are supposed to live because even if these aren't instructions on how we are to live the truth, grace is not limited to situations that we don't want to experience in life. The truth is that sometimes we are innocent, are good, and are faithful, and the beatitudes are also focused on those times because Jesus also said blessed are the meek, the peacemakers, the pure in heart, the merciful, and those are things we are supposed to do, ways we are supposed to live. So it's tempting to think that it's a matter of "if I do this then God will do that for me" but let's keep in mind that these are sayings about God's grace.

I honestly think sometimes these are the part of the beatitudes that we really need to hear because while no one goes looking to grieve, to doubt and struggle in faith, to be bullied or persecuted, the other beatitudes are about what happens when we do everything right, when we live as God asks and it is still not enough. Those types of situations are where and when we often have our crisis of faith and cry out to God wondering why we are suffering.

When we do what we are supposed to do, when we live as people who are humble, innocent, forgiving, and gracious, life can still fall apart. We get overlooked, put down, or walked over when we are meek or humble. We get accused, smeared, despised, and hated despite being pure in heart or innocent. We are merciful and forgiving and that mercy is thrown back at us and we get hurt even more. We try to make peace and nothing changes or it gets worse. It is important to remember that those bad things don't happen simply because we're not good enough, not trying hard enough or for any other reason. The truth is that being meek, a peacemaker, pure in heart, and merciful is important but it isn't always enough to make life good. The truth is that being a person who is faithful and following Jesus doesn't prevent you from being hated and despised. The truth is sometimes when we are at our best and do our best life still turns into the worst.

The good news for us at those times when we do everything right and things still turn out wrong is that God comes to us. The good news is that God responds to the injustice of the world with grace so that those who are humble are given everything. He responds so that those who are merciful receive mercy, so that those who are pure in heart or are innocent, experience God and know the truth, and so that those who are peacemakers are recognized as holy and righteous.

I need to pause for a moment and pay attention to those promises because they seem confusing. Those who are merciful receive mercy. Why would you need to receive mercy if you are merciful? Well quite simply because we learn as we share mercy how much we need mercy in our lives. We discover that our mercy is not enough and we need God's mercy. Those who are pure in heart experience God and know truth and I think this one is probably most surprising because we expect that to just naturally flow because we think that if you are good, you are holy. The fact is that being pure in heart can be a really hard way to live in our world.

That brings me to the peacemakers because we just assume they will be revered and perhaps over time they will be. In the moment they are seen as anything but holy and righteous. That is why God's grace is so important for any who seek to bring reconciliation and peace in our world. It's important to note that the words of Jesus don't mean that we always get what we want. These are words about God's grace and not instructions on behavior with a reward to follow. Remember the peacemakers are not promised that they will see peace, only that others will recognize that they follow God. Those who are persecuted are not promised it will stop, only that God will not forsake them.

The beatitudes are promises, surprising, unexpected, and wonderful promises about God's grace. They are how God's love and care will meet us and answer us in our lives, during the times when we desperately need change and hope and in the times when we are doing what we are told to do and the world is not changing. In faith we are told that God will answer us,

God's grace will touch us when we can do nothing more and be nothing more.

The good news Jesus proclaimed was that God's grace comes to transform us so that the worst of the world does not have the final word. We are blessed in our lives not because of what we do or even who we are. We are blessed because God loves us, God cares for us, and God's grace enters our lives to open a new way, a better way, for us and for the world.

Amen.

Proper 26 (31)
Matthew 23:1-12

Leading As Servants

Halloween can be a fun evening with costumed children going door to door or it can be an anxious and fearful night where fires are set and vandalism takes place. A number of years past an area I served as a minister had seen things get worse and worse on October 31, despite the efforts of police and fire services. They arrested, threatened, and warned each year, and yet the situation became more out of control. Everything came to a head one year when the fire department was trying to put out a blaze in an abandoned building that was in danger of spreading and mischief makers began to throw rocks and debris at them. The fire chief ordered the hoses turned on the teens that night and the next day the community exploded with threats of criminal charges against the teens and accusations of gross misconduct against the fire department.

The police sergeant called everyone together and announced that the status quo could not continue and a solution had to be found. Everyone agreed that the chaos and destruction on Halloween in the community would only get worse unless something drastic was done. The loudest voices called for a dusk to dawn curfew to be put in place and to immediately jail offenders. Those voices declared that there was no other way but there was and what happened instead was something I found incredible to witness.

On Halloween, the community hosted a dance for everyone who attended school, grade nine and up. The local service club provided hot dogs and pop. The off-duty police officers were around — not to enforce the laws but to help make the event happen. School buses went around the shore at dusk with community chaperones and picked up the kids. They also returned them home around ten that night. No one was forced to attend but they all went because their friends were there. They also attended because when they got off the bus at the end of the night every teen got a ticket stub for a drawing the next day at school for some small prizes. The event took some work for the community but many acknowledged it was an enjoyable time they got to spend with the teens. They also have none of the troubles they once had on October 31.

In Matthew 23:1-12, Jesus was warning the crowds about the ways the religious leaders were leading. He condemned those leaders for putting burdens on people and not doing anything to help to relieve the suffering and needs of the people. He accused the leadership of worrying only about their own honor and privilege, their own egos and place in the community. Hearing those words, I think it is tempting to simply imagine the reaction of the crowd as they agreed with Jesus, and nod our heads as well, as we dismiss the religious leaders of the day as being arrogant and close minded. After all, we see them as the opposite of what Jesus asked and called for in his ministry. The problem with that approach is that we point at someone else, we look at another time, and decide that they are wrong instead of listening to what Jesus was condemning and denouncing as he taught. Jesus was focused on the religious leaders of the day and their emphasis on certain things but the real message for us is not in what those people did wrong but in how we, as people of faith, followers of Jesus, are to follow and demonstrate a much different path.

The truth is that all of the things that Jesus accused the religious leaders of, the arrogance, the focus on social recognition and praise, the ignoring of the needs of the suffering around them, are also challenges for us. After all, let's be honest, who among us doesn't like to feel superior or in the know? Which one of us doesn't enjoy being recognized and praised in public? How many of us look at the social problems that cause such suffering — addiction, crime, poverty — and don't think in some way that those people are less worthy, less holy than us?

When Jesus talked about the problems of the Pharisees and others to the crowd and the disciples, he was not merely telling them what not to do but holding up as well how the disciples, how the people of God, are meant to act and be. That is why when I hear the words of our gospel lesson, I can't help but think of that solution to the problem that the community was having with violence and arson among the young people. Our world often calls for us to get tough and take action by exercising authority and control in the face of chaos. Yet, the approach that Jesus spoke about in the gospel lesson took a different approach by calling us to lead as servants.

Let me pause on that point for a moment, because I think sometimes we assume leadership is something that only concerns us if we are elected officials, a manager or employer, or even an officer in the armed forces. Yet the reality is that each and every one of us leads and is looked to as a leader. If you raise children, know children, or even have children around you at some point in the week you are being looked to as a role model, a leader. If you have ever been a coach, a mentor, or even shown someone else how to do something and at anytime you add your voice to a decision being made or help shape something that is happening at work, church, school, or even at home then you are leading others.

The way Jesus called us to be leaders, to share our gifts, to influence the world is by humility and service — a perspective that says what we have been given should be used not to make us greater but for the greater good. If you like that, it is a very Christian perspective because it helps us to understand we are children of God, blessed, loved, gifted, and chosen, and that we live within a world filled with other children of God whom we are supposed to care for and love within our lives. For the way of faith, the life Jesus calls us to live is based upon a humble attitude and actions of service.

In our gospel, Jesus was upset with the arrogance and uncaring actions of the religious leaders around him. He pointed out its hypocrisy and destructive effects and told his followers to exercise humility. Let me be clear here that humility is not about putting yourself down but about putting others first. A humble person is well aware of the great things they can do but also understands that does not make them better or more important than someone else. Humility is not about forgetting your value as a person but recognizing the value in others.

Humility is celebrating the achievements of others even if it isn't as great as your achievements. A humble life does not overshadow others but allows the blessings we receive to bless those around us. When we live as a servant we express, we share, we show in our lives the love and grace and God and they are lifted up, they are cherished, and in what we do they see for themselves the presence of God in their own lives.

It is that perspective, being humble, shifting the focus from us to the other person that can change the world, break patterns of violence, restore hope, and help transform lives. Thinking and acting in the way of Jesus, being a servant, being humble does not place burdens onto others but rather helps them with their burdens. By adopting the way of service, the faithful way, we refuse to be a part of the problem but instead work together for a solution.

I know very well that approach, the way of humility, the Christian idea that we are to be servant leaders, is often criticized as weak, ineffectual, and wrong. The prevailing thought is that real power comes from making others do what you want. It is that we can only succeed when others fail. That might makes right whether that might comes from money, sexuality, power, influence, or authority. We might believe that what we do has to be more important, more worthy, than what anyone else does.

Yet Jesus warned us that those who exalt themselves will be humbled and those who humble themselves will be exalted and he taught that the greatest among us is the servant (Matthew 23:12). If we broaden our perspectives and ask what is best rather than what is best for me we discover the way to transform the world and ourselves in the process. We find that better way Jesus called us to walk and we see the difference that approach, that living, that leadership makes for us and the world.

We can look at history and compare the Marshall Plan that rebuilt Europe after the Second World War and led to an unprecedented stretch of peace on that continent to the punitive measures and reparations after the First World War that brought about an even deadlier and bloodier conflict in less than a generation. One way led to instability and resentment, to anger and sowed the seeds for the Second World War. The other way led to Europe purging the evils that had devastated it and allowed the people to find a better way and indeed to stand up to and reshape themselves in the face of other evils that arose.

We could look at the Truth and Reconciliation Commission in South Africa that allowed that fractured nation to heal the wounds of apartheid and avoid the bloodshed that happened to so many of its neighboring nations in the transition from minority to majority rule. It came not by punishing and vengeance but by coming together to listen, to weep, to shine the light on the evils of the past in a very public way. It came by allowing peace to flourish and hope to take root in the communities, families, and individuals who had been scared and broken by the violence and hatred.

We could also look at our own lives to see the ways that we have known new beginnings because someone forgave us, a hand was offered to us to help instead of hurt or because someone took the time to care for us when we were in need. Those are the times that we knew we were valued and loved, experienced the new start and grace that we hear about in the gospel, began to truly live as God calls us to live.

That is what we see God living out for us in Jesus. Jesus came with the power and authority of God and chose to be a servant. He came to lead and teach not by building himself up but by giving of himself to others. He took what he had and gave it away for the sake of others, showing us the love of God by healing the sick, by eating with the rejected, and coming to the lost and alone. Seeing the value in those who were dismissed as worthless and lifting up the importance of the least was Jesus' way. For Jesus showed in his life the way God calls us to live and his words ring out for us to understand that even when we teach we are still learning, that even when we lead we are still following, even when we are respected we are to respect others.

We are to be servants in this world and lead by our example. We are to show others the way that caring and compassion affect relationships and bring healing and reconciliation. We are to demonstrate in our lives the power and possibility that come from mercy and forgiveness. We are to live the truth that Christian humility and service do not diminish us but makes the world a greater place for all. We are to be the light and love of God in the world not for our sakes but for the glory of God alone.

Amen.

Foolish Or Wise?

"Then the kingdom of heaven will be like..." (Matthew 25:1a WEB). The stories Jesus told, the parables, are stories that help us to understand God's will and way. Each one of them begins with a normal situation, something we can relate to and understand — like a rebellious child, a traveller who runs into trouble, or even someone going out to plant a garden. So that we have no problem hearing what Jesus says and we aren't confused about what he means.

Yet these are not simple stories because as the parable progresses there is a surprise and often multiples surprises within the story, something that catches our attention or that we didn't expect and that point, that place shows us God's grace and love — that the wayward child is welcomed home, that the stranger stops to help, that the seed is sowed everywhere. The surprising or unexpected parts within the story comfort us, encourage us, and perhaps even inspire us to see faith and God's call to us in a new way.

The parable of the foolish and the wise bridesmaids (or virgins) is a parable of Jesus but it is a slightly different than many of the beloved parables that we know so well. This story is still about God's will and God's way but the focus isn't as much on God as on how we need to act in our lives because within the parables we are told about someone who is faithful and someone who is not and while it is easy to see who is who, there is still a surprise within the story, a part that shows us God's will and God's way, in order to help us better understand what God is doing and how grace works in the world.

These types of parables are sometimes called parables of judgment because they remind us that how we act is important.

While we might hear the word judgment and think of someone condemning us and indeed within these stories there is someone who gets it wrong and who we should be like, we should never forget that above all these are stories Jesus tells so we can learn and live more fully as God's people and know God's grace and love in our lives.

That brings us to the first of three parables in Matthew 25 that is often referred to as the parable of the foolish and wise bridesmaids. Biblical scholars are unsure exactly what cultural practices Jesus was referring to in the story but honestly, I think we are told everything we need in the parable to understand what was happening and what was expected.

The bridesmaids were to wait for the bridegroom on the wedding night and escort him into the wedding feast, and that is simple enough to understand. Their job was to wait for him outside and then bring him into the feast so that the wedding celebration could continue. All ten had to wait and it got late. The shadows fell and it got dark. We are told that five of the bridesmaids were foolish because they had no oil and five were wise because they brought oil. That again is easy to follow and we know that what the wise bridesmaids were doing as right because they had prepared and brought oil to light their lamps. What the foolish bridesmaids were doing was wrong because they had forgotten the oil and had none for their lamps.

The bridegroom arrived and the waiting was over. It was time for the bridesmaids to do what they were supposed to do: escort the groom to the wedding banquet. The five bridesmaids with oil light their lamps and the five bridesmaids who were foolish realized they forgot something really important. They asked the wise ones for some of their oil and the five wise bridesmaids told the five foolish bridesmaids "no." The wise bridesmaids told the foolish to go and buy oil for themselves and that answer is surprising.

I say that it is surprising because we always hear about how we need to be generous, share, and give of ourselves. We are told to be people who give, provide, and help. So why wouldn't the wise ones share? Why couldn't they simply give some of their oil to the foolish bridesmaids so that everyone had some? There are two things we need to understand.

First, let's keep in mind what the bridesmaids were supposed to do on the wedding night. They needed the oil for their lamps to escort the groom into the wedding feast and if the wise bridesmaids gave the oil they had away, they wouldn't have enough to do that task. The wise knew they had to refuse in order to get the groom where he needed to go. If they didn't, then they failed in their role within the wedding.

The second thing we need to consider is that perhaps the foolish ones couldn't simply be given the oil because they needed to get it for themselves. In the parable, the image Jesus used was that the oil had to be bought and I think that helps us to recognize that in life there are some things that others cannot do for us. There are certain things that only we can do, certain choices only we can make as we go about our lives because the truth is that we can't borrow faith, or hope, or even love from another person. It just doesn't work that way. Trusting God requires us to give up control and let go. That is something we have to do in order for us to experience what that means. Loving another person requires us to be vulnerable so that we can know and be known.

No one else can love another person for us as that is something only we can do for ourselves. Hope requires us to believe in God instead of ourselves and once more while there are things others can do to help us ultimately only we can believe and have faith. If it helps, think of it this way: We have to pay for faith, for hope, and even love, with our time, our effort, and our choices. No one can simply give those things to us. We are the only ones who can make them happen in our own lives. The truth is that some things you have to do for yourself and no one else can do them for you. Yes, people can support you, they can guide you, they can encourage you, and heaven knows they can even show you. But at the end of the day, you have to be the one to pray, to learn, to follow Jesus in your life. No one can give you faith because faith comes from what you do, how you live, what path you choose to take each and every day. That brings us back to our parable.

The foolish bridesmaids rushed off to buy some oil from the merchants and while it may not seem that important to the whole story, I think it bears noting that the wise showed the foolish what they needed to do. While we may be shocked that the wise bridesmaids didn't give the oil to the foolish, the truth was that they didn't simply abandon them or ignore them in their need. The wise told the foolish what they needed to do and in fact I'm going to suggest that the wise knew that is what the foolish had to do because buying oil from the merchants was what the wise bridesmaids already had done.

The foolish bridesmaids got their oil, lit their lamps, and raced back to the wedding banquet to complete their task they were asked to do, but the door was shut because the groom had already arrived and the wedding procession had moved into the banquet. The foolish bridesmaids pounded on the door asking to be let in and the groom refused to open the door because he said, "Most certainly I tell you, I do not know you" (Matthew 25:12 WEB). That is another unexpected surprise.

The foolish bridesmaids have the oil, they are wanting into the banquet so why wouldn't the groom let them in? After all they had their lamps and they were ready to lead him to the banquet. Except, at this point in the parable, the bridegroom was already in the banquet and the foolish bridesmaids had failed in their task and were too late. That is a disturbing twist to our story because we would like to think we have all the time in the world to believe, to trust, to hope in God. We would like to think we have all the opportunities to do what we need to do as people of faith and all the tomorrows we could ever want to learn and grow as disciples of Jesus.

Except, in truth, we don't have all the time in the world and if we are going to be perfectly honest, all of us know that already. There are things that if we postpone, if we don't do now, then we will never be able to do later. Your child gets older and the chance to teach them how to ride a bike is gone. The estranged family member dies and you can't reconcile with them. The friend you adore moves and you can't go places with them anymore. The opportunity will pass us by, the time will come and go, and the moment will be over because the fact is that there are parts of our life that we can never go back and live again. That all sounds quite discouraging.

Remember that this is a parable with both foolish and wise, and while we are uncomfortable that there are some left outside, let's understand that there are also some who are inside. That is why the end of the parable says be like the wise bridesmaids in your lives. While all of us are uncomfortable with what happens to the bridesmaids who are left outside, Jesus didn't tell this parable to make us lament about how we have failed and fallen short in our lives. No, this is a parable to encourage us to be ready, to do today what should not be put off any longer, and to answer the invitation of the gospel now. This is a call for us to start walking with God today if we have been wondering how to proceed in life. This is a call for us to open our hands and our hearts and to shine in the darkness of this world. This is a call for us to be a better, more faithful, more courageous disciple of Jesus in the world this day.

The time is now for us to be the people God calls us to be. The time is now for us to be generous, to be bold, to be daring, to be faithful, and to share the gospel message in the places where there is fear and worry — where there is uncertainty and pain. The time is now for us to bring the hope, the peace, the love, and even the joy of Jesus to the world, so that the hurting have someone to be with them. We need to bring it so the lost and forgotten see the way home. We need to bring it so that we are in the world being the people God needs us to be for our loved ones, for our neighbors, for our friends, and for our community. We also need to bring it so that we, you and I, will be like the wise bridesmaids and not the foolish ones because we know what God has told us to do and how God has told us to act.

We know that God means for us to be disciples of Jesus and to make a difference here and now, in this place and in this time. When we do, when we are wise and stay awake to and live in faith, then we see and we become a part of the kingdom of heaven that God is making here on earth.

Amen.

Good And Faithful Or Wicked And Lazy?

I have a number of million dollar bills that I keep in my office at the church and before you ask they are not real but rather novelty notes because we don't have banknotes of that denomination in our country. The reason I have them is that when I talk about the parable of the talents to teenagers, I use fifteen of these novelty banknotes to tell the story.

The reason I do that is because in Greek and many English translations, Jesus tells of a master giving talents to his servants and when we hear talent, we think of things like singing, drawing, gardening, sewing, or some other skill that we might have. While that isn't a bad way to look at the parable when we are considering how to use what God has given to us, the truth is that what Jesus is actually talking about in the story is money. If we think of the parable strictly in terms of what we can do rather than what we have been given then we miss much of what Jesus is saying.

A talent for the people of Jesus' time is a certain weight of precious metal worth about nine years of good wages. One servant got 45 years of wages, the second eighteen years of wages, and the third nine years of wages. The truth of the matter is that still doesn't give us anything easy to imagine. That is why I use million dollar bills when I talk to teenagers because if we start talking about five million dollars, two million dollars, and one million dollars this becomes a much different parable. Even the servant who got the least still got an incredible amount. All of that helps us begin to hear what Jesus is teaching.

This story is another judgment parable of Jesus, the second of three from Matthew 25. Like the earlier story of the foolish and wise bridesmaids this is a call for us to examine our behavior and to understand that what we do in our lives is important for our faith. Like the other parables of judgment within the parable there are examples for how we should act and an example of what not to do. While the story of the bridesmaids challenges us to be ready to answer God's call the parable of the talents asks us to look at how we are using the gifts God has already entrusted to us.

Jesus told of a master who went away, called his servants, and gave them some of his wealth. One got five million dollars, one got two million, and the third received one million. Why the different amounts? Jesus explained that each servant got what they could handle so everyone was able to manage what was given to them. That point is important because it all gets dropped into their laps to do with as they see fit. It was a fortune for them to use. Let's not forget that they had only been given what they could handle. They hadn't been given anything beyond their ability to manage. The master hadn't set the servants up to fail but had actually been careful to give them what they needed to succeed. But there was a catch even though it wasn't explicitly stated. The wealth still belonged to the master and at some point he was going to come back and ask for an accounting.

The first two servants used the money. We're not told exactly what they did but they increased the wealth entrusted to them. They had an amount of wealth in their hands, they could handle it, and they increased what they had been given. The third servant, however, decided to bury the amount to keep it safe. As expected, the master returned and called for them to explain what they had done with his wealth. We can almost picture him lining the servants up and saying "So what did you do with my riches?"

The first servant, who received five steps forward and said that he earned five more, and the master was thrilled. He said "'Well done, good and faithful servant. You have been faithful over a few things, I will set you over many things. Enter into the joy of your lord" (Matthew 25:21 WEB). It's important to notice those words: *good and faithful*. The promise was given of more to manage because of a job well done and last but certainly not least the joy of the master. Words of praise, support, affirmation, and actually just what we expect from a servant who does exactly what the master asks, does his work, and has success.

The second servant, who received two steps forward, said he earned two more and the master was as thrilled as he was with the first servant. He said, "Well done, good and faithful servant. You have been faithful over a few things; I will set you over many things. Enter into the joy of your lord" (Matthew 25:23 WEB). *Good and faithful* – the promise of more to manage because of a job well done and last but certainly not least the joy of the master. Words of praise, support, affirmation, and actually just what we expect from a servant who did exactly what the master asked, did his work, and had success. Except there is something familiar about the words the master used.

The master's response to the first two servants was exactly the same even though they were given different amounts of wealth and had different levels of success. That is where we start to see that this parable is about more than money management. After all, we can understand that the master was happy with both using the wealth entrusted to them to make more. It doesn't fit that the master was just as happy with the second servant as the first servant and yet the words that the master said to both servants were word for word the same. All of that helps us understand that the master seemed to be concerned about something other than the wealth — a point that becomes obvious when the last servant stepped forward.

The third servant came before the master and explained that he was afraid of the master and he didn't want to lose any of the money so he hid it away. He was going to return exactly what the master entrusted to him and the master was furious. He called the servant wicked and lazy because he said if he was that afraid of him as his master, then he should have entrusted the money to someone else so at least it would have grown a little during his absence. The furious master banishes the third servant, that isn't really a surprise, but then the master does something unexpected. He ordered the wealth entrusted to the third servant to be given to the first servant. There is no doubt that while this parable mentioned money and finance that money and finance are not the point of the story.

Just like the parable of the bridesmaids isn't about wedding preparations, this story of talents being entrusted to servants isn't about money management. Within the parable, the master reclaimed none of the money that he gave to the servants before he left but rather left it with him and actually hinted he would soon give them even more to look after. The master's concern wasn't about how much they earned, because he was just as happy with both servants who did something with the money given to them, but rather that they chose to do something with the gifts entrusted to them.

When I speak to teenagers about the parable this is the place I like to ask the question of what they think would have happened if one of the two servants who tried to use the money ended up losing some of it. If the servant with five traded it but ended up only getting four back, I ask the teens if they think the master would have been angry or praised the servant for his faithfulness. I think the master would have used the exact same words we find in the text for the simple reason that this parable is not about making money but about being faithful. This parable is about being trustworthy with the things God has placed in our hands. This is where the meaning of this parable really strikes home, because the story stands as a reminder that God has placed great wealth in our hands and God expects us to use those things not selfishly, not to stop God from being mad at us, but faithfully. God expects us to take what we have been given to enrich and expand the gospel itself. God expects us to take our wealth and not hide it away but to use it. God expects us to take what we have been given and give back to the world.

Yes, I am talking about money because that is part of what Jesus was talking about. We are expected to use our money faithfully. We are to give, be generous, and to bring hope and healing with the wealth we have under our control. That may involve giving to the church or charity in order for good to be done; it may involve us using the money directly to buy or pay something for someone else; but it always involves us helping others, giving to others, selflessly. This parable is about more than money management so the expectation of God on us is about more than simply sharing our material wealth. It is also about using the forgiveness, the mercy, the grace, and the love we have been given faithfully, so that we forgive as we have been forgiven, bless others as we have been blessed, and love boldly, freely, and deeply as God loves us. This parable is a call for us to use what we have been given, what comes into our life and affects change not merely our in our own lives but in the lives of those around us and the world itself.

That is the real challenge of this parable because while few of us may have millions of dollars placed in our hands, we have all received riches from God. Within our lives, your life and my life, there are blessings and opportunities and time itself. We have things we can do and we have time that has been given to us. The question each of us need to ask ourselves, the question the parable of Jesus asks is 'How are you using the things that God has entrusted to you?'

In our parable we are shown two examples. Those who have and use their gifts for the glory of God, so that what God gives becomes more prevalent and plentiful in the world. The good and faithful servants who are praised by the master and even more as they enter into a promised joy and new life. Then there are those who hide what they have been given out of fear and worry. The wicked and lazy servant who is condemned and banished from the master's sight and experiences sorrow and regret.

The question for each of us to consider is a personal one. Are you good and faithful with what you have been given? Do you seek each day to increase the kingdom of heaven, the presence of God with what you have in your grasp? Or, are you wicked and lazy, thinking only of yourself and refusing to risk, to go beyond your own fears with what God has entrusted to your care? Make no mistake about it, Jesus calls each and every one of us to faithfully answer God by using our wealth, our gifts, our talents, in a way that brings joy to heaven, furthers the hope and peace of the gospel, and allows us to share even more in what God is doing in our world.

Amen.

Thanksgiving Day
Luke 17:11-19

More Than Thankful

"...Your faith has healed you" (Luke 17:19b WEB). The last line of the gospel lesson for Thanksgiving Day is a confusing end to a story that is easy to follow. There were ten lepers who called out to Jesus for healing. Jesus told them to go on their way for they had been made clean. Of the ten who were cured, one returned to thank Jesus and to praise God for his healing. Jesus then asked the disciples where the others were before telling the former leper to go. Then Jesus said to him, "Your faith has made you well."

I need to be clear that all ten lepers were healed. They all had a terrible disease that affected their lives, that slowly destroyed their bodies, and that kept them separated from their family and friends. There is no doubt in our story that all ten were physically healed. They were all cured of their affliction and in case we missed the part that they were all healed, when the one leper came back to say his thanks, Jesus asked"Weren't the ten cleansed? But where are the nine?" (Luke 17:17a WEB).

There is no doubt in my mind that all ten were relieved and grateful that the burden of leprosy had been lifted from their lives. I expect that every single one of them could not wait to begin a new life and leave all their troubles behind. They rushed to get the clean bill of health and were focused on starting over again now that they were free from the disease that had afflicted them but the one former leper who returned did something that none of the others did. He returned in thankfulness. He came back to Jesus and offered thanks and praise because he didn't simply take the opportunity and move on with his life. He let the experience of being healed change him. I know saying that sounds strange because the lives of all the lepers Jesus heals were changed.

There is no doubt in the story that all ten, every single one of the people afflicted by leprosy and outcasts in society, were blessed by Jesus, cured of their disease, and restored to a new life. They all had a new start, they had, if I can use church language for a second, they had all experienced the amazing grace of God. Yet Jesus made a distinction between the nine and the one who came back. For the other nine went back to their old lives. They put the bad behind them and tried not to think of it again. After all, isn't that what we do with difficult times? We get through them and then don't look back. We breathe a sigh of relief and hope they never happen again. We often act as if they never took place.

Yet one came back and did something that changed everything. No — that didn't change the fact that all ten were healed. They were and there is no doubt in the text about that. Yet we can't ignore the fact that Jesus said that the faith of the thankful leper healed him. That is something that I believe we need to understand as we consider this day and what we are doing. The truth is that the experiences we grow from, that transform us, are the ones where after we have passed through them, we look back and realize that things can't return to the way they were before but need to change. We take the blessings in our lives and use them as an opportunity not simply to escape the bad but bring ourselves closer to God. That is why the single thankful leper was held up by Jesus and Jesus drew attention to his faith. For that man, being cured of his affliction was not simply the way to have life return to normal but being cured was an opportunity to begin a new life.

Today is Thanksgiving. It is a time for us to stop and give thanks for the blessings of God in our lives. Many of us will gather later with family and enjoy a special meal together. During that time we will share in the good things produced by our land and perhaps if you have not done so already you will go around the table and name what you are grateful for in your lives. We all have many reasons to be thankful. We live in a wonderful part of the world, where the land and the seas provide a bountiful harvest. There is incredible beauty in the trees and plants as the cycles of nature progress around us. We are surrounded by family and friends, neighbors, and loved ones who support us in our times of struggle and make our times of joy that much more special. We know that our churches are a holy place and when we come through those doors we can feel the presence of God at work among us.

As Christians, part of our thanksgiving is for us to pause to be thankful for how we have been forgiven and how forgiveness has touched our lives. We hear parables of grace and know the blessings of God in our lives and world and we stop and re-member how grace has changed our lives. Jesus died and rose again and we, each and every one of us are the people whose lives are renewed, transformed, and blessed by the love of God. We have much to be grateful for in our lives but Thanksgiving is not meant to be a time for selfishness where all we do is tally the ways in that we are fortunate and feel smug that we have more than other people. Thanksgiving is not a day when we see how much we have and hope we get even more in the days to come. Thanksgiving starts with us and what we have been given but it has to go further in order to make any difference, real difference, to us and the world around us.

The world needs more than us getting some blessings in our lives. All we need to do is look at the news and know that there is chaos and difficulty in the lives of so many people. There are people still trying to put their lives back together following the floods, the wildfires, and hurricanes that occur in different plac-es. Add to that the horror of shootings and murders that shake communities to the core. Acts of terrorism that occur all too fre-quently not merely in places far away from us but close to him. The places where there are civil wars raging and other areas where neighbor is persecuting neighbor. Not to mention the on-going tensions that seem unending in places like the Middle East and on the Korean Peninsula.

I haven't even touched on the things happening closer to home. The deaths in our community, the illnesses in our fami-lies, the marriage breakdowns, the uncertainty about work or health, or the future, touch us all. Around us there seems to be such great need, such pain and hurt, so much chaos and fear that it almost seems trite and meaningless to talk about what we have been given and how thankful we are. Except we need to be recognizing how we have been blessed and coming to God with our thanks and that will lead us to that curious ending in our gospel lesson.

When we give thanks to God then something greater happen to us. Like the grateful Samaritan, we need to head back to express our gratitude, our thanks, to God then we can allow ourselves to be changed further. We praise, we worship, we connect to God and we open ourselves up to the peace, the hope, the strength, and the guidance of heaven. We start by being thankful and that attitude allows us to receive even more from God — the ability to have the faith necessary to face and make a difference in our hurting world. When Jesus said to the thankful leper that his faith had healed him he was talking about something deeper, something more important, than physical health. Jesus was pointing out that by being thankful and turning to God with those thanks that the leper was allowing that connection, that relationship, that faith to inspire and guide his life. That made the former leper not only healthy but well, whole, certain, because he was walking with God.

I'm not sure about you but I know I need that in my life. Not simply so I can be unselfish and keep what I have been given in perceptive but so that I can be grounded in God's grace, God's love, God's presence, and to face those fears, that anxiety, that hurt in our world. I need that so that my hands can be those that not only receive but also give and I'm not simply talking about passing along things but showing and sharing the hope and peace of God. I am talking about letting actions speak of a truth that transforms the world and allowing words to move people's hearts and lives. Thanksgiving is about seeing the great things in our lives, recognizing them for the gifts they are, and embracing the giver of those gifts so that we ourselves become a gift to others.

This year, I hope each and every one of you takes the time to remember all of your blessings. Recount the good things you have in your life and the good people who are part of your world. Bring to mind all the times that people have been there for you when the days were difficult and remember the grace and love that held you up when you were finding it hard to stand. After all, just because we have had struggles and difficulties, just because there is disheartening and troubling news that doesn't mean that there aren't blessings in our lives. Remember the things that have brought you joy and given you strength. Remember how God's peace and hope and love has touched our lives in expected and unexpected ways. Remember those things and give thanks to God that they are part of your life. Let your hearts be filled with gratitude

This is a day for us to see how we have been blessed and understand how rich our lives are. It is a time to understand that God has been generous with us and in turn calls us to be generous with those around us. It is an occasion to recognize what God has given to us and how we should give to others in the same way. It is an opportunity for us to focus on our blessings and understand how we in turn can be a blessing to others and then, then let that gratitude inform and anchor our faith. As the fall progresses into winter, as you face difficulties and troubles, as life unfolds, you must know that God has not abandoned you or any of us. You must know now and always that we are not alone in this time, that you let your thankfulness, *we let our thankfulness*, move our hands to action and our words to service.

The God who created has blessed us, the God who came among us has saved us, the God who moves within and around calls us to live in faith, to care, to give, to bless others through our lives and to be the reason that others are thankful. For this Thanksgiving we are not merely to be thankful for what we have received but to allow our gratitude to help us see the way that God has opens for us in the days to come.

That is why Thanksgiving to God is so essential for us as Christians. We are not merely grateful people who know we have been blessed by God but know that we can come to God with open hearts and open hands and become the means by which this hurting and uncertain world sees and knows the grace and love of God.

Amen.

Christial the King
Christ the King
Matthew 25:31-46

A Parable Of Comfort And Warning

God cares. I hope that message is not a surprise to anyone gathered here this morning. After all, we sing in the church about God's love for us and read in the Bible that if anyone loves then they know God. We profess that the love of God is most fully seen through Jesus of Nazareth who in his ministry, his death on the cross and by the resurrection demonstrates that nothing, nothing in heaven or earth, can stop God's love from touching our lives. We celebrate in the church that the Holy Spirit is an expression of God's love and the gifts and blessings that the Spirit brings are signs that God cares.

All of that fills us with hope and expectation because the message that God loves us so deeply that God forges a connection through Jesus and the new covenant that cannot be broken and then showers us with blessing and grace, that message, that gospel, changes lives. The good news brings healing and new life, forgiveness and a new beginning to those who hear and believe and as people touched by that grace we understand that we are to love others, to care for those around us. Our lives are to be filled and directed by our love for God and neighbor. We are to be generous, patience, merciful, compassionate people. Jesus tells disciples to love one another in the way that he loves and again I don't think that is not anything new or startling to anyone who has heard the gospel message proclaimed before.

If we know God loves us and that we are to love one another why does everyone seem so surprised by what happens in parable from our reading? Why are the righteous so confused by what the king says to them? Why are the unrighteous dumbfounded by the king's judgment? We could say they just didn't understand that we are supposed to love and care about other people. Yet I think Jesus' words actually push us to a deeper understanding of both God and our Christian calling.

The parable is the third parable of judgment found in this chapter of Matthew's gospel. I know when we talk about judgment lots of different things come to mind — things like guilt, anger, and punishment. But those things aren't the reason Jesus tells these stories. No, these parables, like all the stories Jesus tells, are a call for us to recognize what is important and essential in a life of faith. The other two parables of judgment from Matthew 25, the parable of the foolish and wise bridesmaids, and the parable of the talents, there are people who do what they are supposed to and there are people who don't. The ones who do what they are supposed to — the bridesmaids who were ready for the bridegroom and the servants who used the gifts the master gave to them — are meant to serve as role models. We are supposed to be ready, be active like them and the ones who face consequences in the parables — the foolish bridesmaids whose lamps had no oil so they weren't ready and were left out of the wedding feast or the servant who was lazy and wicked refusing to use the wealth given to him by his master and who got cast out — are examples of what not to do in our lives. This parable, the parable of the sheep and the goats, follows a similar pattern.

At the end of the age everyone will be gathered in front of the king's throne and Jesus says that the people will be separated like a shepherd separates the sheep from the goats. And the king will say to the people on one side "Come, blessed of my Father, inherit the kingdom prepared for you from the foundation of the world" (Matthew 25:34a WEB). We know right away that these are the people we need to pay attention to — they are the role models, the ones who did it right, the example we are to follow as people of faith. And the king says, "For I was hungry and you gave me food to eat. I was thirsty and you gave me drink. I was a stranger and you took me in. I was naked and you clothed me. I was sick and you visited me. I was in prison and you came to me..'" (Matthew 25:34b-35 WEB).

No one should be surprised that those acts of caring and generosity are something that Jesus would want us to do but before we go any further I want us to notice a couple things about what the king praises. The first is that there is nothing that difficult about any of those actions. The king didn't praise the people for doing something that took years of study to figure out or that only was possible once in their lifetime. The fact is that anyone and everyone can feed the hungry, can give to those in need, can welcome, and can visit. We all have the ability to reach out to others, we all have the resources to give some of our blessing away, and we all can open our hearts to help our neighbor.

The second thing to notice is that the king cares about those actions. Think about that for a moment. There is nothing earth-shattering about anything the blessed people had done. These were every day, common expressions of love and care but the king was really taking all of it to heart. The king was taking it personally. That is why the people who were praised in the stories were a bit confused. They did all of those things but they didn't remember the king as being the one they helped. They asked when it was that they did those things to him and the king answered them. "Most certainly I tell you, because you did it to one of the least of these my brothers and sisters you did it to me" (Matthew 25:40 WEB).

While it may be surprising that the king cared about what they did to other people, the truth is that *we get it*. After all, we notice and appreciate the effort if someone is kind, merciful, and helps people we love. Jesus was saying that the most basic actions of loving our neighbor, when we give of our resources, when we offer our time, when we put in the effort to care for others in their need, those are all expressions of faith. When we feed, clothe, visit, when we do all of those things it is as if we are doing those things to God for our generosity, our caring, our compassion toward others are seen and treated by God as an act of worship and love. That point is important for us to keep in mind as we turn to the rest of the parable that is often ignored.

The king said to the others before the throne, "Depart from me, you cursed...; for I was hungry, and you didn't give me food to eat; I was thirsty, and you gave me no drink; I was a stranger, and you didn't take me in; naked, and you didn't clothe me; sick, and in prison, and you didn't visit me' (Matthew 25:41-43 WEB). Those are hard words to hear because while we know that our actions are important, we often overlook that our inaction is a problem. Caring is not simply a good thing but a faithful thing so if we don't care, if we ignore, then we are actually sinning against God. Again, if we think about it, how do we feel about those who ignore our loved ones when they are in need? If your child is hungry or lost and someone turns their back on them — or hurt and in pain and ignored by someone who can help — how do you feel about that person? The parable tells us that is how the king feels.

The people who were being condemned were as confused as the righteous. They didn't ever remember seeing the king in need in any way because they certainly would have helped the king. The king replied, "Most certainly I tell you, because you didn't do it to one of the least of these, you didn't do it to me" (Matthew 25:40 WEB).

Notice the difference in the wording between what the king said to the blessed and the condemned. The ones who were praised were told that it was because they helped the king's family, loved ones, in their time of need and now the ones who were condemned were told the king's family was *anyone in need*. The surprise of the righteous was that the ones they helped were treasured by the king and the surprise of the condemned is that everyone who was in need was treasured by the king.

I think this is the place where we begin to see a bit of the kingdom of heaven because the king took caring personally. Yes, I mean that the king cared but more than that the king cared about what was done to the king's people. Any acts of kindness, any generosity, any caring done to the king's people was taken by the king as if it was done to him. The flip side was, and is, also true. Any time needs were overlooked, people's suffering ignored, the king took that personally as if the person was ignoring and rejecting him. That meant that our ideas about caring may be too small, too narrow, or too restricted. We understand that God cares and wants us to care as well. Yet sometimes I think our sights get set on the big picture while God cares about the little things. We might think that the only people who are really caring are the people who are able to donate the billions of dollars like Bill Gates, or who donate their whole lives to service like Mother Teresa. Yet the expectation God has for us is that we will care in quiet and continual ways. Within our everyday lives in everyday ways, we are to give and serve others, by making sure there is food for the hungry to eat, clothing for the cold to wear, comfort for those in hospital and those who are grieving and even visitors for those in prison. We are to care as God cares and more importantly, we are to care about the people God cares about. God expects us to love without hesitation or restriction.

Let me talk a bit more about that for a moment because there are no limitations around the help that is described in this parable. The food wasn't only for those who were hungry through no fault of their own. The clothes were not for those who were naked because of circumstances beyond their control. The welcome was not because they looked like a nice addition to the community. The visit was not in response to them being unjustly imprisoned.

The king never talked about who deserved such treatment and who didn't but rather whether those who could help did help. The love God asks us to show in the world is a caring and grace filled love that touches lives that are broken and undeserving, and it reaches the lost and the lonely. The love of God that we see lived out through Jesus is a love that changes lives and invites those who experience it to live as forgiven and new people right here and right now. That is the love we are called to share.

Like the other parables of judgment from Matthew 25, that leaves us with a choice to make in our lives because the parable is very blunt and straightforward. A life of faith has to include feeding the hungry, giving water to the thirsty, clothing the naked, caring for the sick, and visiting the prisoner — period. There is no option because this is a requirement and these actions are essential for our worship and service. If we are following Jesus, we are caring for the people Jesus cares about and if we don't we are turning away not merely from what God wants but we are turning away from God.

Are you a sheep or a goat? Do you ignore those in need, turn them away out of fear, or do you care and open your heart and your hands to help? Does the money in your pocket stay there until you want it or do you give some so that others can eat, find comfort, and know that they are loved?

The kingdom of God is not about what we have but about what we give and it is about us seeing and knowing that we and the people around us are loved and treasured by God. When we care, when we are compassionate, when we give of ourselves to those in need, we are not only pleasing God but we are also building the kingdom of heaven here on earth.

Amen.

www.ingramcontent.com/pod-product-compliance
Lightning Source LLC
LaVergne TN
LVHW091205080426
835509LV00006B/843